Trump - Nixon on Steroids
Stay Woke
By

D T Pollard

Follow D T Pollard https://twitter.com/dtpollard

http://DTPollard.com

1

Stay woke! A Constitutional crisis is not caused by someone in power that is in violation, but by those empowered to intervene allowing it to take place. D T Pollard

Stay woke! The United States as we know it may be on the verge of extinction. Over 300 million people are in the process of being mugged in broad daylight and those tasked with protecting us from such blanket grand larceny have invoked a no snitching gang rule due to their lust for power. Our political leaders are intent on stripping us of our wealth, health and voice while enacting self serving policies in the process.

Our loved ones could be sent to shed blood and die in foreign lands to satisfy some political agenda or create a distraction without a second thought. Greed runs rampant throughout the political class and they seek to enrich themselves and their wealthy supporters at our expense. Don't be foolish and think this is about who is more authentically American because of the color of their skin or heritage. The most authentic Americans among us were placed on reservations in order to satisfy so-called larger agendas. Whether you live in the rust belt, Bible belt or on one of the coasts, if you are not among the wealthy predators you are viewed as prey to be stripped, consumed and cast aside. I know "stay woke" is not from the proper King's English, but it means to pay attention because they are coming for you and your only chance is to know what they are trying to do so you can protect yourself the best way you can. Keep your eyes open, your senses keen and your mind sharp because they're coming for you too.

Stay woke because the situation we find ourselves in as a nation and world has been coming at us for years, but now it has finally arrived. People have been emotionally, financially and psychologically battered to the point that many grasped onto the hollow promises of a ranting madman proclaiming that he alone could save them. Little did they realize until it was too late that the only person that false savior planned to rescue was him and his associates by stripping bare those that placed him in power over everything they own with intentions of redirecting it for his own gain.

The nation is being led by a delusional charlatan who is trying to lead a Constitutional Democracy like a despot in charge of a banana republic. The 45th President of the United States has installed the structure of a hybrid monarchical aristocracy rife with nepotism and staffed with plutocrats of the highest order while he indulges in self enrichment through his closely held worldwide business interests. No man has ever been so unknown despite public fame before becoming President of the United States. The 45th President of the United States has a swirl of suspicion floating around him due to Russian cyber hacking interference in the 2016 Presidential campaign confirmed by 17 United States intelligence agencies.

Donald Trump, the 45th President of the United States was the first Presidential candidate in decades who did not release his tax returns. Many trivialize the importance of knowing the sources of money that supports the person that would be President, but it is critical. Money or debt leverage over an individual is a powerful motivator to induce someone to do the bidding of the debt holder and that is not a position the President of the United States should ever be in. Not knowing if there are hidden motivations for a man holding what is considered the most powerful position in the world is uniquely dangerous. Not knowing if the longest standing geopolitical adversary of the United States, Russia, has blackmail level leverage over the President of the United States could be deadly.

The President has unique powers and one of those powers is the ability to declassify classified information by simply telling it to someone else. Apparently, President Donald Trump shared highly classified information with Russian officials, regarding aviation terrorism threats, in the Oval Office on May 10, 2017, one day after he fired the Director of the FBI. The only way the general public knew what President Trump did was through reporting by the media that he hates. Trump would later send out a tweet that he had the absolute right to share classified information with Russia. The intelligence community was aghast because what Trump shared could allow Russia to trace down the foreign sources of that provided that intelligence to the United States and discourages other nations from assisting us in the future. President Trump's loose lips may have put lives at risk. The thickness of the Russian smoke around Donald Trump was obscuring everything else from view, but that does not mean that other things are not happening that we need to pay close attention to because they will outlast Trump as President.

The mistake most decent individuals make is they project their value system upon others and that is a grave mistake when dealing with individuals with far different value sets than those held by what most people would deem decent human beings. The average person would not assume that someone running for public office would purposefully lie, shade the truth or use strategic wording in order to deceive them and get their support only to stab them in the back once they were elected into a position of power. You must understand there are few politicians that talk from their own heart, but they deliver crafted talking points that appear to tell you what you want to hear. You may think you are voting in your best interest when in fact your mind converted what was said into what you wanted to hear. We are no longer in control of those we elect to political office to act in the best interest of voters that placed them in power because they are not working for us any longer.

It requires massive amounts of money to run modern political campaigns and the wealthy donors financing those campaigns demand a return on their investment in getting these politicians elected. The rest of us need to guard against playing the role of gazelles grazing in the grass on a quiet sunny day while a pride of hungry lions are hidden, but prepared to pounce and rip our throats out so they can feast.

You must understand that as individuals we matter little to the top ten or one percent, but collectively what we have contributed to over generations is the prize lusted after. Politicians dare call something you have paid for all your life an entitlement like Social Security and Medicare. Those are not entitlements, that's your money and they want it. There was $2.8 Trillion in the Social Security trust fund and $263 billion in the Medicare at the end of 2015. Source - https://www.ssa.gov/OACT/TRSUM/index.html. Social Security and Medicare are like golden eggs to Wall Street and politicians lustful to shift those funds into the bank accounts of their wealthy supporters in the form of tax breaks. Medicaid spending grew 9.7% to $545.1 billion in 2015. https://www.cms.gov/research-statistics-data-and-systems/statistics-trends-and-reports/nationalhealthexpenddata/nhe-fact-sheet.html . According to the Social Security

Administration. Medicaid is a jointly funded, Federal-State health insurance program for low-income and needy people. It covers children, the aged, blind, and/or disabled and other people who are eligible to receive federally assisted income maintenance payments. https://www.ssa.gov/disabilityresearch/wi/medicaid.htm .

Why do we need to know about these things? We need to know because those trying to redirect what was designed to help us are counting on the general population to be asleep to the details of what they are trying to do to us. Ignorance is the most dangerous condition known to mankind because it enables exploitation. Diseases can kill you, but ignorance can allow crippling of generations through financial and social deprivation.

Social Security and Medicare are easy, look at your paycheck stub, if you still get one, and you will see the deductions for them every pay period. You are paying for future payments back to you once you reach an eligible age to receive them. It's your money. Don't fall for the okie-doke peddled by some politicians portraying Social Security and Medicare like they are some kind of welfare program that must be changed or privatized.

Never get mad with your money, but sadly many have allowed their emotions to be whipped up to a point that caused them to make decisions that may haunt them and their families for generations. We have willingly placed foxes in the henhouse to lead us and now they are planning to feast on us and our efforts. Trump played to the lowest levels of fear to be a driving motivator for making decisions versus what was in the best interest of the individual, many made emotional instead of rational decisions.

Presented with a choice of going to a doctor when you are not feeling well or waiting until you are so sick that you have to go to an overcrowded emergency room, which would you choose? Most people would choose to go to the doctor. What if you were made to dislike the insurance plan that allowed you the ability to go to the doctor because of who made it law and are convince that it should be replaced by some unknown better plan, you may have unknowingly selected the emergency room. Taking away the funds that allow you to go to the doctors instead of the emergency room and giving it to the wealthy is one example of political foxes feasting on us, but how big a meal are they planning? It helps to know how much money we contribute to the federal government every year:

Total Receipts

Funds collected from selling land, capital, or services, as well as collections from the public (budget receipts), such as taxes, fines, duties, and fees.

2016

$2.99 Trillion
Distribution of Total Revenues

Source: http://federal-budget.insidegov.com/l/119/2016#Revenues&s=1c NiL

That $2.99 trillion collected by the federal government is just the beginning. When federal, state and local tax revenues are added together, the estimate is a total of $7 trillion. $7,000,000,000,000 is a lot of money and it can be spent to help the many or the few. We should choose our leaders wisely because our treasure, security and democracy are at risk. During the last election cycle emotions were fanned often in a xenophobic nationalist way to create support for a candidate espousing such views. Desperation drove others to support one candidate over another due to the promise of bringing jobs back to beleaguered areas of the country where many left behind by the new economy were suffering. The Presidential election resulted in the United States being led by the most erratic person ever elected to be President of the United States. Trump is not working for you, but he is working to separate you from your treasure. Stay Woke!

2

At a time after the United States democracy has been attacked by its most formidable geopolitical foe, Russia, we have the most dangerous man in modern history occupying the oval office. The 45th President of the United States is a man wholly unprepared for the job he is tasked to perform. Donald Trump is man with zero prior experience in government. Trump came from a world where his word was final since he was the head of a closely held family run real estate business. Donald Trump was accustomed to individuals following his commands without question because they worked for him, but that is not how government works. Donald Trump probably thought he would not win the Presidential election, but unexpectedly won under a cloud of suspicion due to the interference of Russian interests that attacked Trump's opponent through stolen information and leaked emails.

Since taking office Donald Trump has attempted to transplant his top down autocratic management style from his private business to being President of the United States and it has caused nothing but problems. From the beginning of his Presidential term the Trump White House has been in a state of constant turmoil. Two executive orders issued by the President banning travel from several majority Muslim countries were blocked by federal judges. Trump failed to secure budget funding for the southern border wall he touted constantly when he was running for President. Most disturbing of all was the fact that Trump's campaign and team was under investigation for possible ties and/or coordination with Russia both before the election and after the election. The Federal Bureau of Investigation was looking into potential ties between the Trump Presidential campaign team and Russia before the election to determine if there was coordination in how damaging material hacked and stolen from the Clinton campaign was used against her before the election. The second part of the FBI investigation concerned contacts between Trump team members and Russians after the election and whether they discussed loosening sanctions imposed on Russia by the administration of the 44th President of the United States, Barack Obama.

The first casualty of the Trump/Russia era was his National Security Advisor, General Michael Flynn. Flynn was fired 24 day after accepting the position because he lied about contacts with Russia after saying he did not have such contacts. Flynn told the Vice President of the United States he had no contacts with Russia and the Vice President repeated the story. The White House was told by the acting Attorney General, Sally Yates, that Flynn had misled them and Vice President Mike Pence.

Although the President was informed about Flynn's deception he was allowed to serve as the National Security Advisor for eighteen more days until the fact that Flynn lied about Russian contacts came out in the press and then Flynn was fired. The Attorney General of the United States, Jeff Sessions, was forced to recuse himself from the Russia investigation because he stated during his confirmation hearing that he had no contacts with Russians during the campaign or transition period, but later it was found he did have contact with Russian Ambassador Sergey Kislyak.

Donald Trump was enraged because he could not get his way in the manner he was accustomed to when he was running his private business and began to lash out like a cornered animal. Trump went on twitter tirades and took swipes at everyone from federal judges to the media. Trump attacked and tried to delegitimize the Judicial Branch of the United States government using the bully pulpit of the Presidency. Trump referred to a Federal judge that blocked his first Muslim travel ban as a "so-called Judge". Later Trump indicted he would like to break up U.S. 9th Circuit Court of Appeals, that just happened to be the court the federal judge came from that blocked Trump's travel ban. Trump carried his war against the media from the campaign trail right into the White House. It was very odd to witness a sitting

President of the United States call the media the enemy of the people. There seemed to be very little that Trump liked if it didn't go his way and much of it did not because he discovered that being President was not the same as being king.

Just because Trump was not King did not stop him from banishing those from his presence when they failed to do his bidding. U S Attorney Preet Bharara apparently was investigating a member of Trumps team and was fired by Trump. Then acting Attorney General Sally Yates warned Trump about General Michael Flynn ties to Russia, but when she stated she would not defend his Muslim travel ban, she was fired.

Finally Donald's Trump's ultimate obsession was his desire to be seen as the legitimate President of the United States and two factors ate at him constantly and there was nothing he could do about either of them. The first factor was that Trump could not change was that he lost the popular vote to his opponent former Secretary of State Hillary Clinton by approximately three million votes. The second thing that enraged Trump was the confirmation that Russia interfered with the 2016 election for President of the United States by stealing and then leaking information that was damaging to the campaign of Hillary Clinton. Trump consistently denied that Russia interfered in the election, despite the fact that 17 U S intelligence agencies agreed on that conclusion. Trump decided to attack the intelligence community and continued to denigrate them after he became President. The fact that the FBI was actively investing Russia's interference in the 2016 Presidential election and any ties that the Trump campaign had with possible coordination with Russians to damage the Presidential campaign of Hillary Clinton infuriated Donald Trump. Every news report and public hearing kept the Russian election interference story fresh in the mind of the public. Donald Trump was frustrated with the fact that from his lofty position as leader of the free world he was unable to make the FBI Russia investigation go away. Trump finally reached a breaking point and on May 9, 2017 and fired FBI Director James Comey.

Trump's official account of why Comey was fired had to do with his handling of his investigation of his former Presidential campaign opponent Hillary Clinton. Media reports over the next few days painted a different story that indicated Comey was fired because he would not end the Russia investigation.

Stay woke. We have a man in the oval office with a huge ego, skin as thin as an onion's and desperate for the legitimacy and respect he thinks he deserves. Trump is under siege and who knows what he would do to change the subject. How about shooting cruise missiles into Syria or send an aircraft carrier group to North Korea. What about possibly sending thousands of troops to a war theater to change the subject? A desperate man is a dangerous man and we have a desperate man as President of the United States. Stay woke.

3

Stay woke because the checks and balances the founding fathers build into our federal government structure designed to prevent one branch from running rampant are out of balance. In an age where partisan party affiliation seems to supersede love of country we are discovering how dangerous it is to have one party in charge of both houses of Congress and the Presidency if things go wrong. Politics in the United States have devolved in a high stakes game with rooting interests among the general public as if it is a spectator sport. There is only one problem with voters treating politics like a sport, unlike a team sport, the voters instead of the politicians are at risk.

Those with their grips on the levers of power in the United States of America want your wealth. It is not that they want you sick, silent and broke as a desired outcome, but if that is what it takes to achieve their goals, so be it. Some of you may be thinking that no one you elect could be so cold and cruel, but remember these same people have decided in the past to send your loved ones to be killed, maimed and scarred for life while fighting baseless wars in foreign lands.

"Don't you understand that you people are standing in the way of progress? You know, you people, American citizens that are not a part of the privileged class. Those of you with preexisting medical conditions are dragging the rest of us down with your subsidies that allow you to pay the same for health insurance as someone living a good life. So I'll tell you what I'm going to do. I will fulfill your desire to make America great again by doing something that you have all wanted for years. I will repeal and replace Obamacare with a new plan called the American Health Care Act," the unknown Congressman said to cheers from supporters.

"This plan does not require people that don't want health insurance to get it or have to pay a fine. This plan will allow those with preexisting conditions to still have access to coverage, but states can opt out of the national plan and establish high risk pools. By the way, we are taking over $800 billion dollars out of the plan that was used for subsidies that allowed you sick people to pay the same as healthier people. What's happening to that $800 billion dollars you ask? Well we have a really big tax cut for business and high income earners we need to get passed and that $800 billion dollars will be used to pay for that. You're worried about your premiums increasing? I understand, but you have to realize that for profit health insurance companies can't afford to care for all you sick people at those Obamacare rates and make the profit they require for their shareholders. Why should a young healthy person that does not need as much health care as you pay for your medical costs? Sicker people have to pay more. If you can't afford it than you can still go to the emergency room if you have to because they can't turn you away," the Congressman said.

The previously cheering crowd was silent and fuming at the thought that someone they sent to Washington would leave them exposed to the nightmare of health care of the past that could leave them exposed to sickness, financial ruin and death if they became seriously ill.

"I don't understand why you are so angry? I promised we would repeal and replace Obamacare and here it is," the Congressman said.

The Congressman was last seen bolting from the room as the crowd became increasingly agitated and unruly.

Of course the previous scenario was fictitious, but it reflects the reality of what really took place after voters realized their elected representatives would allow them to pay for a tax cut for the rich with their access to affordable healthcare. It was not difficult for someone to imagine being forced to make choices between paying bills, buying food or going to the doctor like it was in the good old bad old days when insurers could deny health coverage to those with prior medical conditions. While they may not be able to deny those with preexisting conditions, insurers can charge multiple times more to sicker individuals compounded by the massive reduction of Medicare subsidies and loss of the mandate to require everyone to purchase health insurance or pay a fine that contributes to the overall funding of the risk pool. That is the "they want you sick" portion of our current political situation because it suits an overall greater goal in their mind.

Some believe that healthcare should be a basic right to be provided to everyone just like a public highway and other want medical care to be akin to a toll road where heavier users pay a lot more, except there is one difference. Toll roads have a public road option that everyone can use that is supported by tax revenues collected at various levels. Why shouldn't healthcare be like the highway system where someone can choose to pay more for shorter wait times or more coverage, but everyone has a public option to get the health care they need without extra cost? It sounds like a logical approach and now some of the people cheering the loudest at Donald Trump rallies during the Presidential campaign realize they will be hurt the most by the very thing they thought they wanted, a repeal and replacement of Obamacare.

What took place during the 2016 Presidential campaign was a time worn tactic of demagogues that have risen to power, demonization. Trump demonized his political opponents, the media and even the political party whose nomination he was seeking. After Trump convinced his supporters that there was a binary choice between him and politics as usual, he managed to become Presidency by winning through the Electoral College while losing the popular vote.

Donald Trump promised he would drain the swamp of all the politicians dedicated to their own survival instead of making meaningful change on behalf of the American people, but it didn't take long before Trump made his intension clear by his initial cabinet selections. Trump selected a team comprised of a hard-core group of plutocrats including multiple billionaires, multi-millionaires and Wall Street investment bankers. Stay woke, because the flip side of wanting you sick is wanting you broke.

4

While many are waiting with anticipation for the promises made during the Presidential campaign season to come to fruition in the form of greater financial prosperity, President Trump who campaigned as the champion of hard working Americans staffed his cabinet with a large percentage of billionaires and multi-millionaires. Trump's cabinet is the richest in modern history and includes individuals from Wall Street with prior reputations such as the being labeled the "king of debt" or said to have run a foreclosure machine. Trump had the seemingly perfect situation to reach every goal he wanted with the Presidency, both houses of Congress in the control of Republicans and a cabinet ready to do his bidding. Trump's cabinet consisted of the following:

Donald Trump	-President of the United States	$3.7billion
Mike Pence	-Vice President of the United States	?
Steve Bannon	- Chief Whitehouse Advisor	$10million
Reince Priebus	- Chief of Staff	?
Rex Tillerson	-Secretary of State	$330 mil.
Michael Flynn	- National Security Advisor-fired	$8 million
H. R. McMaster	-National Security Advisor	?
Jeff Sessions	- Attorney General	$7 million
Steven Mnuchin	-Secretary of Treasury	$400+mil
General James Mattis	-Secretary of Defense	$5 million
Wilber Ross	-Secretary of Commerce	$2.5billion
Tom Price	-Secretary of Health and Human Services	$13million
Mike Pompeo	- CIA director	?
Alex Acosta	-Secretary of Labor	?

Rick Perry	-Secretary of Energy	$2 million
John F. Kelly	-Secretary of Homeland Security	$4 million
Ryan Zinke	-Secretary of the Interior	?
Sonny Perdue	-Secretary of Agriculture	$11 mil
David Shulkin	-Secretary of Veterans Affairs	$17 billion
Robert Lighthizer	-United States Trade Representative	$18 mil
Dan Coats	-Director of National Intelligence	$4.5 mil
Mick Mulvaney	-Director of the Office of Management & Budget	$2.5 mil
Mike Pompeo	-Director of the Central Intelligence Agency	?
Scott Pruitt	-Administrator of the Environmental Protection Agency	?
Linda McMahon	-Administrator of the Small Business Administration	$500 mil
Nikki Haley	- United States Ambassador to the U.N.	$1.4 mil
Betsy DeVos	- Secretary of Education	$5bil/fam
Elaine Chao	-Secretary of Transportation	$22 mil
Ben Carson	-Secretary of Housing & Urban Development	$10 mil

In addition to the formal cabinet members are the advisors appointed by Trump that are often closer to him and more respected by him than his cabinet officers. Steve Bannon, former head of alt right web platform Breitbart News, is Chief Advisor to the President of the United States. Bannon was given equal status to Chief of Staff Reince Priebus. Bannon was a driving influence early on and his stamp could be seen all over the currently blocked travel bans. Trump brought in even more trusted advisors that set off nepotism alarms across the nation. Trump installed his son-in-law, Jared Kushner, as a senior advisor. Having his son-in-law as an advisor in the White House was not enough of a security blanket for Trump because he also placed his daughter Ivanka, in the west wing as an Assistant to the President. Trump was effectively attempting to create a semblance of his family run real estate business environment in the White House except he was now the head of the United States government.

To say the tenure of Donald Trump as President of the United States has been like no other would be an understatement. Trump created more self-generated distractions in less than four months in office than other POTUS created during a four year term. Trump engaged in twitter wars with the press, Senators and a movie star that took his place on a reality show, but don't get too distracted. While everyone was trying to figure out what Trump was up to on Twitter he was busy rolling back environmental regulations, insulting our allies and recommending a budget that cut funding for meals on wheels among other things. Trump rolled out an outline of a tax cut that would be a windfall for the rich. President Trump also found time to help push a health care bill though the House of Representatives that would remove 24 million America off health insurance that utilized Obamacare. It became obvious that President Donald Trump was a master magician with the ability to distract with antics with one hand while preparing to pick your pocket with the other. President Trump even found time to roll back higher nutrition standard for public school lunches championed by former First Lady of the United States Michelle Obama.

The Republican controlled House of Representatives was busy as well operating under the cloud of confusion created by the President. In addition to passing a health care bill that would increase insurance costs and leave 24 million Americans uncovered by health insurance, they came for the paycheck of hourly workers. The Working Families Flexibility Act was passed with only Republican votes in the House of Representatives. The Working Families Flexibility Act allows employers to offer time off instead of overtime pay. President Trump, the self anointed champion of hard working Americans, supports and said he would sign the legislation if it landed on his desk in its current form. While the crafters of the proposed law stated it is the worker's choice to take time off instead of overtime pay, the truth is that hourly workers have the least amount of leverage ever and could be pressured into taking time off instead of overtime pay in order to keep their jobs.

The Fair Labor Standards Act of 1938 was signed On Saturday, June 25, 1938 by President Franklin D. Roosevelt. Work life as we know it was largely created by the FLSA:

- The 40 hour work week was created

- Overtime pay of 1.5 times per hour worked over 40 hours was implemented
- Child labor laws were implemented
- The weekend as we know it was created

Almost 80 years after its implementation along comes a Republican crafted bill designed to strip away protection from exploitation from some of the most vulnerable working in our society. There should have been fierce debate and reaction to The Working Families Flexibility Act, but with so much Trump generated turmoil taking place that sucked all the oxygen out of the room over the Russia investigation, health care bills and North Korean standoff that everything else flew under the radar. We can't allow bright shiny objects to distract us while other legislative actions are being slipped under the radar rolling back social, economic and environmental gains won over decades prior. The political period we are living through is a wrecking ball for progress gained for protection of the individual American. We need to stay woke and see through the smoke screen and protect ourselves or do you want Wednesday off instead of overtime for working Saturday? Stay woke.

5

Trump was engaged in a chaos Presidency and like most authoritarians; he wanted no opposing voices to be heard so the idea of actually changing the First Amendment of the Constitution relating to free speech was raised. Using language that is foreign to the average American, Trump spoke about changing libel laws. Why would President Trump want to change libel laws, because he does not want anyone or any institution challenging what he says, exposing what he does or using journalistic sources to present information to the public they would otherwise not know about? So what do libel laws have to do with the First Amendment of the Constitution that may need to be changed to do what Donald Trump wants. First let us review what the 1st Amendment of the Constitution of the United States says:

Amendment I (1791)
Congress shall make no law respecting an establishment of religion, or prohibiting the free exercise thereof; or abridging the freedom of speech, or of the press; or the right of the people peaceably to assemble, and to petition the Government for a redress of grievances.

Source:
https://www.senate.gov/civics/constitution_item/co
nstitution.htm#amdt_2_(1791)

Every aspect of the 1st Amendment is an affront to Donald Trump. Let's get back to Libel. Libel is defined as a published false statement that is damaging to a person's reputation. Donald Trump went to war with the press early on and remained at war with the press throughout the Presidential campaign and his Presidency. Trump singled out individual reporters and directed the ire of his supporters at them during various campaign rallies, but his war with the press was a crusade to erode the credibility of legitimate news reporting operations. Trump did not like the way print and broadcast news outlets reported on him and his activities as a candidate and as President of the United States. Unlike a dictatorship the United States has a free press protected by the 1st Amendment of the United States of America. During the campaign Trump railed against the so-call dishonest press and even labeled some news outlets as fake news. Once he became President Trump floated the threat of changing libel laws. Donald John Trump, of all people, was insinuating that he was having his reputation damaged by news organizations reporting what he was actually doing while President of the United States.

During the discussions around what would be required to change libel laws they way Trump envisioned, would require a change in the 1st amendment since freedom of the press is protected by the Constitution of the United States.

The odds that the 1st Amendment would be changed are low, but the fact that a sitting President of the United States would consider something that would require changing the first amendment to spare his authoritarian ego is chilling. Suppression of a free press is a hallmark of nations like North Korea, Saudi Arabia and Iran. Given the despotic tendencies of President Donald Trump, and his apparent fondness for reviled international strongmen like Russian President Vladimir Putin and President of the Philippines Rodrigo Duterte, he probably dreams of unquestioned power. There is only one thing hampering Trump from being the all powerful and unquestioned ruler he desires to be and it this pesky democracy protected by the Constitution of the United States that limits his power. Just the thought of Donald Trump talking about redoing libel laws after he led the birther movement against former President Barack and accused him of not being born in the United States for years is laughable. After becoming President, Donald Trump tweeted that the 44th President of the United States wiretapped Trump Tower and called

President Obama a bad or sick guy, now that may be a case for libel.

As was said previously the 1st Amendment of the Constitution of the United States is Donald Trump's nemesis. Not only does Trump take issue with freedom of speech and press, he has a problem with freedom of assembly. All of the massive protests that erupted after Trump's election and inauguration were decried by Trump as unfair or he characterized them as put on by a few paid protestors. Dissent and free speech are not things Trump tolerates well. During his years in private business it is reported that people in his employment signed nondisclosure agreements as a regular course of action.

Here we are people. We are living a live test of what happens when you drop a man with all the known quirks, insecurities and background of Donald Trump into the role of leader of the free world. The question is why are we here and why did voters place the future of the United States into the hands of a man with so many seemingly obvious flaws that they seemingly ignored.

President Trump does not want your voice to be heard. Stay woke!

6

What drove that portion of the electorate to vote a political novice like Donald Trump into the Oval Office? Some tried to provide simple answers like racial hatred. Others stated economic frustration and some said a combination of the two, but it is not that simple:

After two hundred and forty years of huddled masses yearning to be free coming to America by air, land and sea, the makeup of the United States was changing to the point that a period of transition to a minority majority has begun and it will be painful for many. The United States is projected to become a majority minority population by 2044 according to the United States Census Bureau, https://www.census.gov/content/dam/Census/library/publications/2015/demo/p25-1143.pdf.

Majority minority means that more than half of the population in the United States will belong to minority groups other than non-Hispanic Whites. Some in the White population already felt forgotten, put upon and unrepresented and that is why the make American great again and take the country back rallying cries gained so much traction.

Many characterized the election of Donald Trump as a kind of primal scream from White American telling the liberals and elites that they do matter, but that was overblown. As the United States becomes a nation that moves into a new phase that actually reflects the realization of the dream of the Constitution and Dr. Martin Luther King, Jr. with a rich multicultural population all striving to achieve their version of them American dream. Instead of promoting a vision of how everyone in the country can all rise together, Trump pushed a dream based upon a memory of the past where one group was dominant over everyone else. That society existed for most of the history of the United States a sovereign nation. After hundreds of years of anyone other than White men and their families being able to fully enjoy the full bounty this great land had to offer, other groups were beginning to assert themselves and rising up the economic ladder. It is not to say that it was purely a racial issue at play, but it became a class and educational divide that was fracturing along racial and even geographical lines.

How sharply divided the nation was became apparent when various networks covering the 2016 presidential election displayed their election maps. Donald Trump won a wide expanse of votes across the southern and middle of the United States. Hillary Clinton captured the West and East coasts. Inside the individual states themselves was a similar pattern, but the states largely showed Clinton winning urban areas and Trump sweeping most of the vast rural expanses. The results was an Electoral College vote victory for Donald Trump by 74 electoral votes, but a popular vote win for Hillary Clinton of almost 3 million votes. Trump became President, but the candidate that was the choice of the voting public by a considerable margin lost due to where her votes were cast.

Although Trump supporters and surrogates repeatedly touted that he won in a landslide, nothing could be farther from the truth. Other's claimed Trump had a sweeping mandate to push through an aggressive agenda, but that was a dubious claim. It can be said that Donald Trump became President by losing the popular vote by the largest margin of anyone else in history."

The last sentence of the prior section points out one of the issues driving Trump to the brink. Donald Trump is obsessed with being the biggest, the best and the most loved in his mind, but Trump could not change history. Being President of the United States and pulling off what could be the biggest upset in political history was not enough to satisfy Trumps ego and it began to push him to further to the edge. The thought that more voters selected his political opponent than him on Election Day was unacceptable and caused Trump to invent wild conspiracy theories and outright fabrications that called his rationality into question. The first things that incensed Trump were observations made by the press and others that his inauguration crowd size was smaller than former President Barack Obama's attendance. Comparison photos taken from the same place clearly showed more people at Obama's inauguration and Trump became unhinged. Trump went to war with the media over inauguration crown size. It seemed to be lost on President Trump that the real victory was that he actually had an inauguration while his Democratic opponent for President, Hillary Clinton, attended the ceremony as a former First Lady.

The second issue that seemed to be endlessly on Trump's mind was the unchangeable fact that Hillary Clinton garnered almost 3 million more votes than Donald Trump. In fact Clinton earned more votes than any Presidential candidate ever, except for Barack Obama in 2008. Of course in the United States we select Presidents based upon the Electoral College and not the popular vote:

Donald Trump was elevated to the position of leader of the free world overwhelmingly against the will people expressed at the ballot box. Republican Donald Trump lost the popular vote to rival Democrat Hillary Clinton by over 2.8 million votes nationwide, but he surpassed the Electoral College requirement of 270 Electoral College votes needed to become President of the United States.

The states of Florida and Pennsylvania were won by Donald Trump by a combine margin of approximately 200,000 votes, but accounted for 49 electoral votes that were enough to ensure that Donald Trump would secure the Electoral College requirement of 270 electoral votes. Clinton ended up with almost a 3 million vote popular vote victory and that meant the statement that "all men are created equal" in the second paragraph of the United States Declaration of Independence does not apply to voting for President. The 200,000 voters in Florida and Pennsylvania, who could be argued, selected the next President of the United States, votes counted 14 times more per person than the almost 3 million more Americans that voted for Hillary Clinton. The amount of people that voted for Clinton over Trump would comprise a city population larger than Chicago, Illinois. Millions more Americans voted for third party candidates, so we have a President that had millions more vote against him than for him, but Americans live with the results of elections in the system we have, the Electoral College.

Americans must trust that a newly elected President would recognize a result in which he lost the popular vote by millions would be sensitive to the need to signal respect for the concerns of all citizens. A President must move from candidate of just his supporters to President for everyone, but Donald Trump did not do that. Trump continued his us versus them attitude and even as President he held campaign style victory celebration in areas that heavily supported him. During his first 100 days as President Trump failed to travel west of the Mississippi River and didn't leave the United States. It was as if President Trump pretended the west coast didn't exist, but he made time for numerous trips to what he called the southern White

House, his Mar-a-Lago resort in Palm Beach, Florida. Donald Trump was conducting his Presidency as if he only represented his core supporters instead of the entire country.

The final proof that President Trump could not ignore his bruised ego over losing the popular vote was his shocking claims that up to 3 million illegal votes were cast and if it was not for that he would have won the popular vote. There was zero objective evidence for Trump's bizarre claim and it was the type of claim no one expected from the President of the United States. No one truly understood Donald Trump's obsession with inaugural crowd size and popular vote loss, except when combined with the cloud of Russian interference during the election it was clear that the thing gnawing at him were questions of his own legitimacy as President. Trump hated the idea that questions of if he won due to interference by Russia in the election were magnified due to his large popular vote loss. Trump was the legitimate President of the United States, but the cloud of Russian interference dogged him to no end. The bombshell of an ongoing investigation that also was seeking to discover if there was coordination between the Trump campaign and Russia to damage Hillary Clinton's campaign was dropped by the Director of the FBI in an open Congressional hearing and it lit a slow burning fuse in Donald

Trump. Trump went into full rage and vengeance mode over the Russia investigation. How did we get here with Russian officials laughing and slapping backs in the Oval Office the day after President Trump fired the Director of the FBI who was leading the investigation in the Trump campaign ties to Russia? Stay woke.

7

During the 2016 Presidential election the United States suffered its most devastating attack ever from the Russian Federation and not a single bullet or missile was fired. The attack from Russia was a new age cyber strike meant to sow chaos and doubt over the results of our Presidential election. Russia attacked the foundation of our democracy. The target of the hack was the campaign of former Secretary of State Hillary Clinton who headed the Presidential ticket for the Democratic party.

Just as The Democratic National convention was due to begin, a stolen email scandal exploded onto the scene as hacked emails exposed that Democratic National Committee was biased against Senator Bernie Sanders during his primary battle against former Secretary of State Clinton. Due to the email leaks, Democratic National Committee Chairwoman Debbie Wasserman Schultz tendered her resignation due to be effective at the end of the Democratic National Convention. The stolen email scandal continued in one form or another all the way up to the actual election itself.

Trump openly encouraged Russia to find Hillary Clinton's 30,000 deleted emails after a hack into the Democratic National Committee email system was linked to probable Russian hackers. Later, hackers accessed the email account of

Clinton campaign chairman John Podesta and the stolen emails were released through WikiLeaks.

Trump seized upon information contained in Podesta's email and used them like they were critical operations research material created by his campaign. Trump even rejected the determination from multiple United States security agencies that Russian interests were behind the hacks of email systems of Democratic Party interests.

The interference by Russia in the United States Presidential election was like nothing ever seen before and after it was examined further it was much more that just stolen email. It was determined that Russia embarked on a wide ranging campaign that included fake news being disbursed widely to potential voters with social media used as a valuable distribution channel. Trump supporters were quick to point out that there were no evidence that voting machines were tampered with or that vote counts were changed, but the fact remains that Russian interference caused negative information about Hillary Clinton to be placed in front of potential voters that would have otherwise not been there. The fact that vote totals were not changed through voting machine tampering may have been a moot point because voters make decisions based upon the information in front of them. While Donald Trump created plenty of problems for himself such as the vulgar remarks about his behavior with women he made on a bus years ago that were unearthed and broadcast on news stations around the world, he didn't have help digging holes like Hillary Clinton did with Russia spreading real and fake negative information against her, but karma came calling for Donald Trump.

Donald Trump praised the onslaught of negative information released by Wikileaks against his opponent Hillary Clinton during the Presidential campaign.

"This just came out. WikiLeaks! I love WikiLeaks!" Republican Presidential candidate Donald Trump said at a rally before the election as he held a document with damaging stolen information on his opponent Hillary Clinton.

Trump's glee over how much the information hacked by Russians from Hillary Clinton's campaign was helping him has definitely changed. It has been said that revenge is a dish best served cold, but in Trump's case it is being serve white hot and it's not clear who is dishing it out. Trump's love affair with Wikileaks has soured as he finds himself embroiled in what must seem like a recurring nightmare over possible collusion with Russians by his campaign during the Presidential election and possibly afterwards. The specter of Russia is everywhere Trump turns and he can't escape it. Donald Trump created a bed of hot coals that he is lying on and he can't even use his old tactics that worked in private business like confidentiality agreement, oaths of loyalty and firings. When viewed in isolation those tactics sound more like those of a mob boss than a President of the United States. Something else Trump praised during the election came back to bite him after he became President.

Trump was furious at FBI Director James Comey after he held a press conference and did not recommend charges against Hillary Clinton after concluding an investigation into her use of a private email server and handling of classified information when she was Secretary of State. Trump was not shy about expressing his displeasure over Comey's decision, but his tune about Comey changed when the FBI direct sent a letter to Congress on October 28, 2016 that possibly additional Clinton emails were discovered on the laptop computer of her assistant Huma Abedin's husband, disgraced former Congressman Anthony Weiner. Comey's letter came 11 days before Election Day and early voting was underway. Trump pounced on the renewed doubts raised by Comey's letter over Clinton's trustworthiness. Trump's campaign had flattened out and sudden he had new energy. Trump stated that Comey had redeemed himself with his courageous move. President Trump's admiration for FBI Comey evaporated on March 20, 2017 when the former FBI Director testified before the House

Intelligence Committee and did not support Trump's claim that former President Barack Obama wiretapped Trump Tower. Comey then dropped a bombshell on everyone when he said:

"I have been authorized by the Department of Justice to confirm that the FBI, as part of our counterintelligence mission, is investigating the Russian government's efforts to interfere in the 2016 presidential election and that includes investigating the nature of any links between individuals associated with the Trump campaign and the Russian government and whether there was any coordination between the campaign and Russia's efforts. As with any counterintelligence investigation, this will also include an assessment of whether any crimes were committed," James Comey – Director of the Federal Bureau of Investigation.

That was the moment that President Donald Trump knew he had a problem and his efforts to try and extricate himself, at best, or distract from the issue went into overdrive, but Trump couldn't run from Russian ties. Trump reluctantly fired his first National Security Advisor, General Michael Flynn, because he supposedly lied about contacts with Russians and was caught speaking with Russian officials about sanctions President Obama leveled on the nation for interfering in the 2016 Presidential elections. Numerous Trump campaign and transition members were caught not disclosing meetings or discussions with Russians until they later admitted so. Those in addition to Flynn who later admitted to meetings, discussions or links to Russian interests are Trump's former campaign manager Paul Manafort, Attorney General Jeff Sessions, Carter Page, Trump associate Roger Stone and son-in-law/advisor Jared Kusner.

Trump's anger over the fact that he could not use all his powers to control circumstances boiled over and he lashed out and fired FBI Director James Comey one day after former acting Attorney Sally Yates, who Trump fired, testified about how she warned the White House about General Michael Flynn's lies about Russian contacts.

Donald Trump is a powder keg ready to explode at what many others would ignore, but to him may be a major slight. One train of thought was when Comey made a reference in an open hearing that it made him mildly nauseous to thing his letter may have affected the outcome of the Presidential election. Some think this set Trump off and he saw it as a dig at his legitimacy as President and reinforced Hillary Clinton's claim that Comey's letter cost her the election and thus elected Donald Trump. Trump took the glass is half full point of view and thought Comey disrespected him and was saying Trump would not have won the election were it not for his late campaign letter about possible new Clinton emails. Trump fired Comey who was leading an investigation into Trump campaign ties and Russia and immediately comparisons to Nixon and Watergate sprang forth. The second thing that started was the question began to be posed was did Trump obstruct justice.

The main reason given for Comey's firing was his handling of the prior investigation into Hillary Clinton's handling of classified emails, but the next day in a nationally televised interview, Trump stated that the Russia investigation was on his mind when he decided to fire James Comey. The smoke around Trump and the Russia investigation was so thick as to be blinding, but not thick enough to stop other things from happening that almost slipped under the radar.

During the confusion, Attorney General Jeff Session reversed an Obama administration policy that relaxed harsh sentences for nonviolent drug offences:

May 10, 2017
MEMORANDUM FOR ALL FEDERAL PROSECUTORS
FROM: THE ATTORNEY GENERAL~
SUBJECT: Department Charging and Sentencing Policy

This memorandum establishes charging and sentencing policy for the Department of Justice. Our responsibility is to fulfill our role in a way that accords with the law, advances public safety, and promotes respect for our legal system. It is of the utmost importance to enforce the law fairly and consistently. Charging and sentencing recommendations are crucial responsibilities for any federal prosecutor. The directives I am setting forth below are simple but important. They place great confidence in our prosecutors and supervisors to apply them in a thoughtful and disciplined manner, with the goal of achieving just and consistent results in federal cases.

First, it is a core principle that prosecutors should charge and pursue the most serious, readily provable offense. This policy affirms our responsibility to enforce the law, is moral and just, and produces consistency. This policy fully utilizes the tools Congress has given us. By definition, the most serious offenses are those that carry the most substantial guidelines sentence, including mandatory minimum sentences.

There will be circumstances in which good judgment would lead a prosecutor to conclude that a strict application of the above charging policy is not warranted. In that case, prosecutors should carefully consider whether an exception may be justified. Consistent with longstanding Department of Justice policy, any decision to vary from the policy must be approved by a United States Attorney or Assistant Attorney General, or a supervisor designated by the United States Attorney or Assistant Attorney General, and the reasons must be documented in the file.

Second, prosecutors must disclose to the sentencing court all facts that impact the sentencing guidelines or mandatory minimum sentences, and should in all cases seek a reasonable sentence under the factors in 18 U.S.C. § 3553. In most cases, recommending a sentence within the advisory guideline range will be appropriate. Recommendations for sentencing departures or variances require supervisory approval, and the reasoning must be documented in the file.

Memorandum for All Federal Prosecutors

Page 2
Subject: Department Charging and Sentencing Policy

Any inconsistent previous policy of the Department of Justice relating to these matters is rescinded, effective today.1

Each United States Attorney and Assistant Attorney General is responsible for ensuring that this policy is followed, and that any deviations from the core principle are justified by unusual facts.

I have directed the Deputy Attorney General to oversee implementation of this policy and to issue any clarification and guidance he deems appropriate for its just and consistent application.

Working with integrity and professionalism, attorneys who implement this policy will meet the high standards required of the Department of Justice for charging and sentencing.

1 Previous policies include: Department Policy on Charging Mandatory Minimum Sentences and
Recidivist Enhancements in Certain Drug Cases (August 12, 2013); and Guidance Regarding § 851
Enhancements in Plea Negotiations (September 24, 2014).

Source: https://www.justice.gov/opa/press-release/file/965896/download

In the midst of the fog created by Trump after he unexpectedly fired Director of the FBI, James Comey, Attorney General Jefferson Beauregard Sessions II, rolled back flexibility on federal drug sentencing guidelines and went back to harsh minimum sentences for drug crimes that result in people rotting in prison for years over nonviolent drug offenses. Jeff Sessions answered the question Trump was asking the African American community during the Presidential campaign, what the hell do you have to lose if you voted for him. Prisons are filled with Black inmates that get much stiffer sentences for nonviolent drug offenses. The following paragraph in Sessions' memo sums it up:

First, it is a core principle that prosecutors should charge and pursue the most serious, readily provable offense. This policy affirms our responsibility to enforce the law, is moral and just, and produces consistency. This policy fully utilizes the tools Congress has given us. By definition, the most serious offenses are those that carry the most substantial guidelines sentence, including mandatory minimum sentences.

Stay woke!

8

We are being taken on a ride and the conductor with his hand on the throttle is in charge of a bullet train without emergency brakes. Donald Trump is the President of the United States, but he is operating like a crime boss. Trump likes to do deals over dinner in dark restaurants, hang out at his resort in Florida and extract loyalty oaths from those in his inner circle. Donald Trump also likes to move up to the edge of the law and beyond if required. One prime example was the way Trump viewed the calls for him to release his income tax return.

Tradition means nothing to Trump. Just because over the decades every Presidential candidate had released their tax returns meant nothing to Trump and since it was an expectation, but not a requirement, he did not do it. Trump completed the required financial disclosures to the Federal Election Commission and that was it. Trump said he would release his tax returns once an IRS audit he said was in progress was over, but after winning the election he said he would not produce his tax returns. As with everything else in Trump's world, his word is conditional, tactical and transactional as are his relationships with those in his immediate circle. It seems the only safe positions in relation to Donald Trump are through blood. Anyone other than family could be thrown overboard if required in order to save Trump himself.

Being in Trump's orbit is a dangerous business for individuals regardless of the positions they hold. Anyone from a National Security Advisor, acting Attorney General or Director of the FBI is instantly disposal. The most disturbing aspect of the situation we find ourselves in is that anyone is acting surprised at all, particularly Republican politicians and Trump supporters.

It is often said that hindsight is 20/20, but foresight is x-ray vision. Republicans, who now protect, support and kiss the ring of Donald Trump after he became President felt far different when he was running for the office. It would be malpractice not to revisit how we got here and compare what was projected would happen, at least by this observer to what actually developed after Trump took the oath of office. What follows is a frozen in time snapshot of sentiment about Trump written right after the election in November 2016 contrasted to what has taken place:

"Text of President Trump WTF – November 2016 – D T Pollard

I watched in disbelief on the night of November 8, 2016 as vote totals began to grind to a halt in Florida and later Pennsylvania and Wisconsin. Like everyone else I knew, I mentally said WTF, but I also had three other thoughts.

During the campaign Donald Trump stated at various points in time that he wanted to ban Muslims from entering the United States, build a wall along the United States border with Mexico and prosecute Hillary Clinton if he became President. Trump started his Presidential run by stating the Mexico was dumping its worst on the United States in the form of criminals and rapists although he assumed some of them were good people. Trump said he would put together a deportation force that would round up the eleven million undocumented immigrants and send them back where they came from.

Trump was recorded on a live microphone moment with an entertainment show host, recounting how he attempted to have sex with a married woman while his new wife, Melania, was pregnant.

Trump said in crude terms, "I did try and fuck her. She was married ..." among other statements about the episode, but it was something else he said while being recorded that set off a firestorm.

"When you're a star, they let you do it. You can do anything," Trump said.

When asked to what extent he meant.

"Grab them by the pussy. You can do anything," Trump said.

Trump was no teenager when the recording was made. Trump was fifty-nine years old. There was no question it was Trump who said those things because the audio was of a video when he was on a bus taking him to a soap opera television show taping. Video of the bus pulling up, parking and Trump stepping off the vehicle left no doubt about him being the one that spoke those words. After the recording of Trump was broadcast, over one dozen women came out and accused Trump of sexual harassment or sexual assault.

Donald Trump conducted a scorched earth of a campaign that left many offended that were outside his target audience. Trump also went to war with the media. By the time the campaign was over Trump had offended women, the disabled, Muslims, Hispanics, African Americans, veterans and families of fallen military members, but he still won. One group that Trump did not offend was White working class citizens, he pandered to them.

Fast forward six months from the election and President Donald Trump was still the same as candidate Donald Trump except he wielded the power of the office of President of the United States. While Trump was not caught on video in another vulgar, sexist rant like he was years earlier, there was no indication that his attitudes had changed. Candidate Trump's twitter attacks now came from the President of the United States and had the power to move financial markets or cause individuals, organization and institutions he attacked many problems. Trump never made a turn to become more Presidential and still attacked those he saw as opposing his agenda. Trump was embroiled in chaos before he became President and brought all that into the White House with him.

One other thing had not changed about Donald Trump and that was that nothing Trump did caused his core supporters to waver in their support for him.

Trump went back to old school politics. Donald Trump went to economically depressed areas of rural America decimated by years of job losses due to shifts in the economic landscape. Industrial jobs that ran under the power of non college educated blue collar workers and provided solid middle class lifestyles have disappeared as the world economy shifted. Technological changes caused many jobs to go away due to automation. Globalization cause many well paying blue collar jobs to disappear as United States based manufactures yielded to the pressure to compete with their competitors that shifted to lower cost offshore production.

What has happened in Pennsylvania, Wisconsin and Michigan is not unique. The rust belt as it is called is not unique because the same shift in industry has occurred nationwide. The small town in Texas where I grew up is dramatically different that it was thirty or forty years ago. The well paying blue collar jobs that were located in the industrial area of town are largely gone or greatly reduced in number. Many of the companies were manufacturing locations of larger concerns and production was shifted to other areas nationwide or worldwide. Some companies ceased operation altogether. The pattern that occurred in my home town was replicated across the nation. The truth be told, it is more difficult than ever for non-college educated workers to make a living wage whether they are located in urban or rural areas. In rural areas it is even more impactful because of the greater scarcity of jobs in general for residents to get in order to make ends meet.

The lack of good paying blue collar jobs means there is no work for blue collar workers regards of their race, religion or gender, so why did Trump focus upon the White segment of the blue collar workforce? The answer was simple. By focusing on disaffected White voters Trump was able to use two motivations to either vote for him or against the existing political class, a need for jobs and anger at the status quo. Hillary Clinton, in the mind of Trump supporters represented the status quo that had failed them and the existing Republican Party power structure was also seen in the same light.

Trump pulled a page from the Republican Party of 1928 when it put out the following flyer in support of Presidential nominee Herbert Hoover.

A Chicken *for* Every Pot

THE Republican Party isn't a "Poor Man's Party." Republican prosperity has erased that degrading phrase from our political vocabulary. The Republican Party is *equality's* party— *opportunity's* party— *democracy's* party, the party of *national* development, not *sectional* interests—the *impartial* servant of every State and condition in the Union.

Under higher tariff and lower taxation, America has stabilized output, employment and dividend rates.

Republican efficiency has filled the workingman's dinner pail — and his gasoline tank *besides* — made telephone, radio and sanitary plumbing *standard* household equipment. And placed the *whole* nation in the *silk stocking* class.

During eight years of Republican management, we have built more and better homes, erected more skyscrapers, passed more beneficiary laws, and more laws to regulate and purify immigration, inaugurated more conservation measures, more measures to standardize and increase production, expand export markets, and reduce industrial and human junk piles, than in any previous quarter century.

Republican prosperity is written on *fuller* wage envelops, written in factory chimney smoke, written on the walls of new construction, written in savings bank books, written in mercantile balances, and written in the peak value of stocks and bonds.

Republican prosperity has *reduced* hours and *increased* earning capacity, silenced *discontent*, put the proverbial "chicken in every pot." And a car in every backyard, to boot.

It has *raised* living standards and *lowered* living costs.

It has restored financial confidence and enthusiasm, changed *credit* from a rich man's privilege to a *common* utility, *generalized* the use of time-saving devices and released women from the thrall of *domestic drudgery.*

It has provided every county in the country with its concrete road and linked the highways of the nation into a *unified* traffic system.

Thanks to Republican administration, farmer, dairyman and merchant can make deliveries in *less* time and at *less* expense, can borrow *cheap* money to refund exorbitant mortgages, and stock their pastures, ranges and shelves.

Democratic management *impoverished* and *demoralized* the railroads, led packing plants and tire factories into *receivership,* squandered billions on *impractical* programs.

Democratic *maladministration* issued *further* billions on mere "scraps of paper," then encouraged *foreign* debtors to believe that their loans would never be called, and bequeathed to the Republican Party the job of *mopping up the mess.*

Republican administration has *restored* to the railroads solvency, efficiency and par securities.

It has brought rubber trades through panic and chaos, bought *blocos,* the prices of crude rubber by smashing *monopolistic* rings, put the tanner's books in the *black* and secured from the European powers formal acknowledgment of their obligations.

The Republican Party rests its case on a record of *stewardship* and performance.

Its Presidential and Congressional candidates stand for election on a platform of sound practice, Federal vigilance, high tariff, Constitutional integrity, the conservation of natural resources, *honest* and *constructive* measures for agricultural relief, sincere enforcement of the laws, and the right of *all* citizens, regardless of faith or origin, to share the benefits of opportunity and justice.

Wages, dividends, progress and prosperity say,

"Vote *for* Hoover"

Paid for by a member of the Republican Business Men, Inc.

Those wishing to see similar advertisements in other New York papers may send cheques to the Republican Business Men, Inc., 4 West 40th Street.

GENERAL COMMITTEE
George Henry Payne, Chairman.

Trump didn't promise a chicken for every pot, but was pushing good paying blue collar jobs for every town as he targeted rural America. Trump would then pin the blame for the loss of the jobs that disappears on the North American Free Trade Agreement that was signed by President Bill Clinton, husband of his opponent Hillary Clinton. The second villain in the loss of middle class blue collars jobs in the rust belt were the others that came in and took opportunity away, illegal immigrants. A deportation force, the south border wall and tariffs on products coming back into the United States from companies that relocated production out of the country were easily sold on the campaign trail.

Trump's war against the media, the establishment and the others attracted support from fringe elements with White supremacist agendas. Trump was not always swift in distancing himself from those with less than stellar views of anyone that was not White. Over time Trump's support was a stew composed of many components and although he won votes from all aspects of American society, his voting block was overwhelmingly White.

Trump didn't win by a blowout in the election and his vote total was less than Mitt Romney's in 2012. Clinton lost the election in the electoral while winning the popular vote nationwide by over 600,000 votes. Clinton received almost five million votes less that President Obama and that is the real reason Donald Trump won. Hillary Clinton was unable to motivate Democrats to vote for her in the numbers they voted for President Obama. To determine why Democrats didn't come out in enough numbers for Clinton to win can't be determined because she lost by relatively small margins in traditionally Democratic rust belt states.

If there was nothing but the Clinton campaign to consider an analysis would be easier to pinpoint. Two letters from the director of the FBI to Congress about Clinton's emails from a private server while she was Secretary of State during the final days of the campaign knocked her off stride while it energized a lagging Trump campaign. The second issue that dogged Clinton was the emails of her campaign chairman's released by Wikileaks after a probable Russian hack. In any case the United States woke up with President elect Donald J. Trump on Wednesday November 9, 2016, but what did it really mean?

Trump's core supporters are giving President Trump a long leash to deliver on his jobs promise. Trump has met with leaders of many different industry sectors, but a lot of that was public relations. Trump spoke of rebuilding the infrastructure of the United States, but nothing has been proposed in the way of an infrastructure project. Trump final popular vote loss margin to Hillary Clinton was near 2.8 million votes and causes Trump to reflexively snap whenever the subject comes up. Donald Trump continued his war with the media and called them the enemy of the people with the power of the Presidency behind it. As for Russia interfering in the United States 2016 Presidential election, it has grown into a counter intelligence investigation on what happened and if there was coordination between Russians and the Trump campaign by the FBI. Trump fired the Director of the FBI on May 9, 2016 and in a televised interview he said the investigation was on his mind when he made the decision to fire then Director of the FBI, James Comey. Two Congressional investigations into Russian election interference were ongoing. Lastly a Special Counsel was appointed to run the Russia election interference investigation.

Just as during the campaign, Trump still does not admit that Russia interfered in the 2016 Presidential election despite multiple ongoing investigations into the matter.

3– November after election

Trump was President elect of the United States and he had promised jobs, mass deportations, a southern border wall and prosecution of Hillary Clinton if he won. The thing is Trump was a surprised as everyone else in the United States when he won. A televised shot of Trump's team as they watched the election results come in showed disbelief on their faces and not expressions of expectations being fulfilled.

Trump had something else in common with Herbert Hoover other than big promises to his supporters. Trump had Republican control in both houses of Congress just like Hoover and wealth disparities like Hoover did when he took office. Within eight months of Hoover taking office the Great Depression struck. As a point of interest there is one more interesting parallel between Trump and Hoover, neither man had ever held elective off before becoming President although Hoover had served in federal government appointed positions. All of this is not to say that Trump will end up like Hoover, but the similarities are striking.

Trump is like the dog that chased a car and latched onto it only to realize he was now hanging on for dear life. Trump's means justifies the end campaign strategy was now generating heartburn as all of those groups he savaged during the campaign along with their sympathizers marched in the streets nationwide protesting his election as President of the United States. American flags were burned. Effigies of Trump were dragged in the street and used as a piñata. Trump's first reaction was to tweet that the protesters were professionals and being unfair to him. The next morning Trump sent out a more moderated tweet about people protesting to express how much they care.

It seemed that the newly elected President in waiting seemed to dismiss the vitriol he spewed toward various segment of American society during his extended run for the highest office in the land. With his defeated opponent gaining more actual votes than he did to become President, Trump was faced with the prospect of half the voters in the nation he will be sworn to serve opposed to his pronounced policies.

So what will Trump do? He seems to be boxed in between what he sold to his supporters and political reality. Trump quickly walked back part of his staunch total repeal and replace of Obamacare in favor of keeping some of the more popular provisions. How long will it take for Trump voters to disconnect from him as his broken promises mount? Trump was selling a return to an earlier time when industrial jobs were plentiful across the land and a certain group was on top. I already lived through Trump's Great America and remember it well.

Donald Trump admitted after he became President that he felt like the dog that caught the car and found out he bit off more than he could chew. In April 2017 Donald Trump stated that he thought being President would be easier than his old job. Donald Trump did not look kindly on all the protests that came after his inauguration, but he did little to unite a country where millions more people voted for his opponents than for him.

Trump's border wall that he turned into a campaign chant of building it with Mexico paying for it is dead in the water. No funding for Trump's border wall is in the current budget and Mexico's President firmly stated they will not pay for it. Donald Trump did step up efforts to expel undocumented immigrants by relaxing what crimes someone could be deported for even if they were not serious. As for Trump's promise to repeal and replace Obamacare on day one, it resulted in one failed bill and I bill that passed, but has no chance to pass as is in the Senate.

"When I was young this was a different country, fast forward fifty years and things have changed drastically. Diversity in the United States is taking hold and the big man could be of any race or may be a woman. A few months ago I was walking through a retail establishment and overheard an older man make a comment that no one cared about you if you were a White male, cue the entrance of multibillionaire Donald J. Trump as the proxy champion for a sizable portion of the population who feel they have been forced out of their rightful positions in American society.

That's right; Donald Trump, a multi-billionaire real estate and entertainment mogul who was born in New York City, New York won the Republican nomination for President of the United States with a message largely based upon xenophobia. Trump's message of keep them out and send them back tapped into a deep reservoir of frustration that had built up over five decades as the United States is poised to become a majority minority population by 2044 according to the United States Census Bureau, https://www.census.gov/content/dam/Census/library /publications/2015/demo/p25-1143.pdf.

Majority minority means that more than half of the population in the United States will belong to minority groups other than non-Hispanic Whites. Consider the timing of Donald Trump's Presidential bid. Barack Obama, the first Black President of the United States was nearing the end of his second term in office and the western world was engaged in a fierce struggle with the Islamic extremist terror group ISIS. Given the environment this was a very serious time and to many it called for very serious people to step forward to run for President. Donald Trump was not considered to be a serious candidate for President, but to the shock of many, he drew huge crowds at campaign appearances, leading the pack of Republican contenders for President in the polls and caused panic within the ranks of the Republican Party. Amazingly Donald Trump managed to position himself as the anti-establishment champion for those feeling unrepresented in their desire to return America to a state they felt existed in the past when the bounty and opportunity of this nation was available for those who were here legitimately. A kind of America for Americans train of thought was at play. There seemed to be a sentiment that many are in the country that should not be here, but were taking opportunity away from others more deserving because they, for lack of a better term, are more authentically American. Trump addressed the festering issue of illegal immigration as his first priority and set the agenda that the rest of the Republican field for President were forced to address on his terms.

Many of the more traditional Republican candidates for President were blindsided and must have felt like they were trapped inside some type of bizarre reality show nightmare orchestrated by one Donald J. Trump. Years of political experience suddenly became a liability regardless of political party affiliation because of the framing Trump put in place. Trump employed a simple strategy that cast everyone from the media to other candidates speaking out against him as the establishment bent on silencing the voice of his supporters. Some entities felt they were immune from Trump's wrath due to their position in the hearts of conservative Republicans, but they discovered that was a mistake. Fox News was shocked at the outcome when Donald Trump effectively went to war with the organization after it hosted the initial Republican Presidential debate. Trump felt he was not treated fairly and lashed out against the network and arguably its most well liked news personality. Ultimately Fox News found itself being shoved in the same corner with the rest of the dreaded media by Trump and his supporters stood with Trump. It seemed that Donald Trump was coated with Teflon® because nothing he said or did seemed to matter from criticizing war hero Senator John McCain to making questionable statements about Fox News personality Megyn Kelly. As the media and political pundits sat by completely baffled, Trump's poll numbers continued to rise after each controversy they thought would bring him down. Not even his battle with a gold star family that lost a son in war stopped Trump. A leaked video in which a 59-year old Trump was recorded admitting that he tried to have sex with a married woman while his new wife was pregnant and that he felt entitled to grope women because he was famous failed to disqualify him with his supporters.

The real question is what was really going on! The answer is simple. Donald Trump was brilliantly executing target marketing to an underserved audience and it may have been an exercise not designed to win the Presidency, but to expand Trump's elite business brand downward to the mainstream, possibly for a television network venture. There was only one problem with Trump's gamble, he defeated Hillary Clinton and was elected President of the United States. Trump and his team seemed to be caught by surprise and scrambled to regain their footing because there was a huge task in front of them to assemble a governing team before he took office. What kind of governing team would Trump assemble? Would Trump staff his inner circle with that demonstrated he was going to be a President that reached out and considered the concerns of the fifty percent of the population that voted against him. Trump's Chief of Staff choice of Reince Priebus seemed logical as he was head of the Republican National Committee. Priebus knew Washington and the political players involved. Trump made a simultaneous selection in Trump campaign CEO Stephen K. Bannon as Chief Strategist and Senior Counselor to the President. Trump stated that Bannon would have equal status with Priebus. Many do not know who Steve Bannon is. Bannon is the executive chairman of Breitbart News. Brietbart News is a website that is aligned with the alt-right. The alt-right is a group with right-wing ideologies. In general the alt-right is in opposition to multiculturalism, immigration and political correctness. Bannon has been described in some corners as a White Nationalist and even a White Supremacist. Many of those marching in the street will see Trump's pick of Bannon as him giving them the middle finger.

Trump built millions of loyal fans and followers by tapping into their latent frustration with the unstoppable momentum of change in the social, economic and demographic shifts in the United States. This was a pretty much a no lose situation for Trump, but why was it happening and how we got here blew the lid off an ugly division in America as some thoughts that were previously shared in private by like thinking individuals were being aired publicly around the world. In the end would this help us or hurt us as time went on.

After months in office Trump is still fighting campaign battles, reliving his election win and still exploiting the cultural divides that put him in office. Trump seems to have no interest in operating as the President of all Americans, but behaves as if he is President of only those that voted for him.

One example of Trump's lack of interest and even disdain for some that opposed him when he declined to attend the annual White House Correspondence. Trump skipped the White House Correspondence dinner and went to a campaign style rally in Pennsylvania where he took shots and the so-called liberal elites assembled in Washington D.C., including the media that Trump seemed to loath. Many remarked that it was surreal to witness a sitting President of the United States spew such vitriol about other Americans and institutions.

The first rule of fishing is to use the right bait to attract what you want and Trump started by throwing out a big chunk of red meat in the form of solving the illegal immigration problem, particularly along the almost two-thousand mile border the United States shares with Mexico. Trump did not delve deep into bothersome details or technicalities, but went with a solution easily visualized by his target audience, a wall. Never mind the various impediments to building a wall along the border between United States and Mexico such as cost, terrain and private land ownership, Trump knew that illegal immigrants, particularly from Mexico, were the new scapegoats for much that has upset the status quo in the minds of his potential supporters. In order to really sink the hook he took no chances and decided to vilify illegal immigrants more by labeling some as criminals and rapists dumped upon the United States by the government of Mexico. The media waited for his seemingly outrageous comments about Mexican illegal immigrants to trigger the implosion of Donald Trump's fledgling candidacy, but the reverse occurred and his poll numbers began to rise.

The traditional media that was based in large urban centers seemed perplexed at the positive response to Trump's brand of bombast that it deemed incendiary. Political pundits took the position of wanting trump to get out of the way so they could get on with the business of covering serious politicians running for President. That turned out to be a grave mistake for mainstream news organizations. Initially the condescending attitudes they had in regard to Donald Trump showed on their faces and his supporters could see it as well. Slowly the realization began to set in with the traditional media that there was a large segment of the American voting public with a vastly different view of the world than it had. Who were these people that began to show up by the thousands at Trump events? Take into consideration that the voting rate in the last United States Presidential election was under sixty percent. Republicans lost the last two Presidential elections and although they took control of both houses of the United States Congress, the mid-term voting rate was less than thirty-seven percent. The prior voting rates means that over forty and sixty percent of the voting eligible population of the United States stayed on the sidelines while others elected the leaders of the nation. That meant that millions of eligible voters basically decided it did not matter who or which political party was in charge of leading the nation forward because they felt there was not a significant difference between either major party. Years of political gridlock, infighting and talking points without tangible results that rewarded all of the conservative fervor and energy expended over the past several years dating back to before President Barack Obama was elected in 2008 took its toll. Despite the birther and Tea Party movements along with the sound and fury they created, Barack Obama won a second term in office. Regardless of the resolve exhibited by Republican elected leadership two of the signature lines in the sand drawn by conservatives were crossed as both National Healthcare and same-sex marriage are now laws of the land. What we have is a large group of disaffected Americans feeling they were sold a bill of goods that were never delivered and they had a leadership vacuum. Nature abhors a vacuum and in stepped Donald Trump who seemed like a red sports car among a fleet of drab gray sedans.

Trump looked, talked and acted different than other politicians. Trump openly said what others thought or hinted before him, even if it was considered politically incorrect. Donald Trump was a New York born multi-billionaire who dealt in luxury real estate yet many of his ardent supporters seemed to be the last people that would support an East Coast plutocrat, but that seeming Achilles' heel was turned into strength. Trump managed to instantly turn his weakness to his advantage by selling himself to potential supporters as their insider, their rich guy and their plutocrat. Trump told the curious masses attempting to determine why he would be the right person to champion their cause and that he was the best person to represent them because he was not owned by special interests due to his enormous wealth and self-funding of his campaign. At the same time Trump was making a pledge to finance his own campaign he painted his competitors as beholden to lobbyists and special interests because they accepted campaign contributions. Trump became the everyman's billionaire advocate with a remedy for what is wrong with America. As the saying goes, he maybe an asshole, but he's our asshole.

Another test that Trump had to pass was to demonstrate that his Presidential campaign was serious and not a celebrity publicity stunt and that would come as time passed. The final hurdle for Trump was proving how he would speak to the world on behalf of his followers. Many Trump supporters felt lied to, used and ignored by more mainstream politicians in both parties. After marching, holding rallies and voting for their conservative favorites with few positive results to show, they took their votes and went home. Many Trump supporters felt that they were looked down upon by elites in American society. Fame worship, less than wholesome lifestyles and pursuit of wealth at all costs are values being pushed in this modern America to the dismay of Trump boosters who felt they were witnessing the moral fiber of the country deteriorate before their eyes.

Donald Trump passed the threshold of durability to prove to those behind him that he was not running a show candidacy by remaining in the race and leading in the polls. In fact Trump seemed to be supporting the agenda of his supporters at the cost of his personal business interests. Trump sold the Miss Universe Organization including Miss USA and Miss Teen USA after backlash due to comments about Mexican immigrants that caused NBC Universal's NBC, Univision and Televisa to refuse to broadcast the competitions. Some retailers removed Trump products from their stores. Some groups cancelled events previously booked at Trump owned properties most notably ESPN and NASCAR. Trump was unbowed and fired back forcefully calling for a boycott of a major retail chain. Trump characterized some of the event cancelations as opportunities to make more money by retaining deposits posted to reserve the venues that he could now rent to others for additional profit. Trumps willingness to meet power with power on behalf of those who felt they lacked someone willing to take tangible hits on their behalf was a breath of fresh air. As the media pounced and pounded on Trump they quickly began to realize something was going on that was more fundamental, attacks on Trump were being viewed as attacks on his sizable block of followers. The media took notice and decided it was time to attempt to understand what was happening instead of dismissing the Trump phenomenon out of hand. Why was Trump resonating while the predicted Republican favorites seemed to have shrunk in stature when held up in comparison?

Donald Trump had something that only one other candidate had in recent memory had, Ross Perot, a level of wealth that inoculated him from concern about consequences from the positions he espoused, but that's where the comparisons between Trump and Perot end. Perot was a solution driven individual and employed charts to illustrate his explanation of how he would solve the country's various problems. Trump did not bother with such details like Perot did to get his point across. Trump's secret to political success at that point was his ability to mainline the thoughts of his supporters and express them out loud without a political correctness filter. What his supporters said in hushed tones in public or out loud to each other in private settings, Trump said loudly in front of television cameras, hot microphones and on social media. While his supporters would not dare utter their true feelings in public for fear of being vilified or losing their jobs, Trump did not have that fear because he was the person that did the hiring and firing and he had it all on video.

Trump merged his reality show persona where he fired and hired candidates competing with each other on various projects with his real life business persona and they seem to be the same person. Trump caused a crisis inside the Republican Party because he did not implode, fade or quit, but instead had increased his lead to double digits. Trump defeated his Republican rivals and became the Republican nominee for President.

President Trump has failed on candidate's Trump's promise to build his big and beautiful border wall along the southern border of the United States. There were two things that were guaranteed response lines at Trump rallies. Lines calling for the immediate repeal and replacement of Obamacare and building a wall along the border the United States shares with Mexico always got candidate Trump's rally attendees going. During the campaign Trump always said that Mexico would pay for the wall. Trump's border wall ran into budget reality and the obvious realization that he had no power to compel another sovereign nation to pay for a united States construction project, particularly one in which the nation requested to pay had its citizens insulted by the requester. It was estimated that Trump's wall could cost anywhere between $12 to $20+ billion dollars. Trump then asked Congress for taxpayer funding of his wall with the caveat that Mexico would reimburse the United States later. President Trump has been a failure on delivering his most ardent campaign promise of building a southern border wall.

Donald Trump spent years spearheading the birther movement in an attempt to delegitimize former President Barack Obama as not being born in the United States and therefore not eligible to be President of the United States. The birther movement failed to prove its point, but it did cause the first Black President to show his papers in the form of his short and long form birth certificate proving he was born in the state of Hawaii. President Trump has continued his assault on former President Barack Obama by trying to wipe out his legacy. Trump rolled back several Obama executive orders including climate change protection, protection for women workers and protected lands.

President Trump's most shocking assault on the 44th President of the United States came when he accused Barack Obama of committing a felony by wiretapping Trump Tower while Obama was still President. Trump found his most lethal personal attack on President Obama fell flat with few people backing him up, but Trump would not relent. Finally, intelligence official publically said there was no evidence that former President Obama wiretapped Trump Tower. Trump was not pleased about a lack of support for his unsubstantiated claim against his immediate predecessor as President.

While his core supporters stood firm with Trump, some of those who voted for Trump because they wanted him to deliver on his promise of improving their economic situation, but didn't buy into his cultural agenda are beginning to peel away as turmoil continues around his administration.

6– November after election

Trump threw down the gauntlet on several fronts starting with illegal immigration. Building a two-thousand mile long wall along the border of the United States and Mexico is simply one aspect of Trump's plan. Deporting up to eleven million illegal immigrants and their children, even if born in the United States, was also part of Donald Trump's immigration plan. The mass deportation aspect of his immigration plan was met with huge amounts of skepticism and deemed unworkable and was even called un-American, but Trump cited a precedent for his plan. Donald Trump invoked the name of President Dwight D. Eisenhower and reminded or in most cases made Americans aware of a program initiated in 1954 with the despicable name of Operation Wetback. Trump never referred to the prior deportation program by name, but it reminded everyone of some of the actions that took place in this nation's history that are difficult to imagine happening now. The illegal immigrant deportation program that took place under President Eisenhower's watch was in response to an influx of illegal immigrants from Mexico due to not enough Mexican farm laborers being able to enter through a sanctioned program endorsed by both governments.

Operation Wetback sent multiple teams of border patrol agents out to round up illegal immigrants who were handed off to Mexican officials who then deported them into central Mexico. Estimates range from 1.3 to 2.1 million people that were deported to Mexico under Eisenhower's plan. Now it came as a surprise to many that such a program ever existed in the United States, but it really occurred. The program was not some flawless execution of a simple relocation strategy. Abuse and even deaths occurred due to the deportation process. Now fast forward to the current time and the leading Presidential candidate among Republicans is advocating removing 11 million illegal immigrants from the United States. The practicality of Trump's plan is very low from a cost, implementation and humanitarian standpoint, but that's not the point. The point of Trump's plan is that it is what his base wants to hear and feel he is the only candidate with the guts to say it.

It has been long held that anyone born in the United States is a citizen, that is the basis of the 14th amendment of the United States Constitution, but Donald Trump wants to change that. Trump and some others on the right feel that birthright citizenship is a strong incentive for illegal immigrants to enter the United States and have a child that is automatically a citizen at birth. The unfortunate term "anchor babies" has been attached to children of illegal immigrants born in the United States and are said to cement the ability of those here illegally to remain. Trump is dictating terms and setting the agenda that the rest of his more mainstream opponents have to play by to compete with him. Other candidates have to be careful when they attack Trump because his ideas and proposals are those of his supporters. Calling

Trump's positions outrageous or ridiculous would be insulting his support base at the same time and that would not bode well for any candidate wishing to inherit Trump's base should he falter at some point along the line.

Donald Trump sees himself as voicing the frustration and anger of an overlooked and unrepresented slice of America, the hardworking Americans that are looked upon as being throwbacks to an earlier time in the nation's history. Many Trump supporters are not seen as sophisticated, educated or progressive enough to understand and accept the evolving trends rippling through America. In a society that is increasing multicultural, sexually liberated and religiously indifferent it is understandable why some feel left out who hold more traditional views when it comes to their ideas of how America should be versus how it is.

Trump's group is angry with the state of the country and with what they perceive as failed leadership. Looking back over the years the social fabric of the nation has shifted and those who feel they are not positioned to enjoy this nation as their parents and grandparents did are bitter. A lot of the resentment Trump supporters feel is not merely because of their current and future prospects, but they perceive their futures were either given away in bad trade deals with other countries or stolen by some other less deserving group. In their view Immigrants, minorities were on the rise at the expense of Trump supporters who consider themselves the real hard-working Americans. As other movements stole the spotlight such as Black Lives Matter in response to police killings of Black men, many in Trump's cobbled together group of followers simmered in relative silence, but they are silent no longer.

Donald Trump seems to be the unlikeliest of figures to play the role he has assumed, but if you examine his strengths, this environment played right into his hands. Basically Trump was feeding an ignored audience with a cargo ship load of red meat that other candidates were afraid to touch. Trump did not need to be a President, Governor or member of Congress to advance his career. This Presidential run was an experiment for Trump and if it failed he would still be a multi-billionaire with a thriving business enterprise, so he can touch every third-rail issue out there without fear of repercussion.

President Donald Trump wants to add 15,000 additional immigration agents in order to speed up deportations of undocumented immigrants. Whether Trump's immigration policy develops into a full-fledged deportation force remains a question, but his broadening of the offenses for which undocumented immigrants has been broadened. As people saw their loved ones deported for nonviolent offenses it had a chilling effect on reporting of some types of crimes by undocumented individuals, including rape and domestic violence in some areas out of deportation fears. Part of Trump's plan to increase immigration enforcement was to enlist local police forces nationwide to identify undocumented immigrants during the course of their routine law enforcement activities, but many cities across the nation objected. City and some state leaders stated that their local law enforcement personnel were not going to be converted to immigration officers and doing so would cause many people to stop cooperating with law enforcement and make their cities less safe. Trump wanted local law enforcement to check the immigration status of individuals as they went about their daily intervention actions like traffic stops.

Trump went to war with municipalities refusing to agree to participate with Trump on immigration. Trump threatened what he called sanctuary cities, with withholding federal funds because they would not agree to his demands. The state of Texas passed a state law that required cities to assist federal immigration officials or be fined for each time they refuse to cooperate. Trump seemed hell bent on ramping up his deportation program to keep a promise he made to his loyal base.

7– November after election

Not only was anger present in Trumps support base there was also fear. ISIS had supplanted Al Qaeda as the top terror threat against the west. ISIS emerged out of the chaos in Syria and Iraq. ISIS was trying to establish an Islamic religious state across the Middle East, referred to as a caliphate. To be clear ISIS' vision was not shared with all Muslims and their methods to achieve their goals are very violent and bloody. Beheadings of westerners had been seen worldwide and no nation seemed to be immune from their wrath from Russia to France. ISIS downed a Russian airliner with a bomb concealed on the airplane killing over 200 passengers on board. On Friday November 13, 2015 ISIS operatives orchestrated a night of terror in Paris, France that left 130 people dead in multiple attacks across various location that included guns and suicide bombers. We are currently at war against an ideology that can spread around the world via social media instantly. Now the person next door can be self-radicalized while sitting in front of a computer screen. ISIS was changing and often referred to by multiple names ISIS, ISIL and IS, but their ability to project terror worldwide was not in question. The main problem that occurs when a terror group has roots in a particular religious faith is for those outside that religion to keep a separation between the true tenants of the faith and those that use elements of that religion as a basis to obtain their goals by violent means. Islam is not the only faith that has been twisted by some practitioners to justify the commission of violent acts that have occurred in almost every faith throughout history. The greatest danger we face currently would be to allow the fight against ISIS to become positioned as the western world against Islam instead of the western world versus Islamic terrorists in the name of their twisted interpretation of Islam. All it really took was a tragic event to occur in the United States with ties to Islam to open the doors to a near explosive backlash against Muslims if not handled carefully. Reaction to an event that occurred on December 2, 2015 when a man and his wife gunned down 14 of his coworkers in an office building in San Bernardino, California was swift when it was reveal that the attackers were of the Muslim faith. The gunman and his wife were later killed by police in a hail of gunfire with the aftermath broadcast on live television.

United States citizen Syed Rizwan Farook and his Pakistani born wife Tashfeen Malik were Muslim and the shockwaves across the nation were immediate, although it was not immediately clear if they were members of any organized terror cell or self-radicalized. As time went on it became clear that there were definite signs of extreme preplanning and self-radicalization. The massacre consisted of 14 people at a county health department Christmas party and was the largest number of lives taken in a mass shooting since the Sandy Hook Elementary School shooting in December of 2012. As the identity and religion of the killers became known everyone held their breaths for reaction from the country at large and political leaders in particular. While some political leaders including President Obama delivered nuanced responses to the San Bernardino tragedy with messaging designed to remind the frightened populace to be careful to separate radical terrorists from peaceful members of a mainstream religion in their condemnation of a terrible act of hate, Donald Trump did not bother to walk a fine line.

Trump employed the nuclear option and advocated a temporary total ban on all Muslims entering the United States until authorities could get a handle on what was going on. The reaction to Trumps Muslim ban was harsh, immediate and worldwide. Trump's Republican rivals piled on and thought that finally "the Donald" had gone too far and imploded his campaign from within. Even the greatest, the late Muhammad Ali, released a statement reminding everyone to not paint all Muslims with a broad brush colored by those presenting a peaceful people and religion under a twisted banner of hate. As shock and revulsion spread within the Republican Party and from almost every corner of the world, the media and Trump opponents in the United State held their breath for poll results reflecting the effects of his Muslim ban remarks. To their shock, Donald Trump's poll numbers remained untouched by his Muslim ban remarks. Trump maintained a double digit lead over his nearest rival and had been in the lead for months on end. Core Trump supporters did not recoil away from Trump and once again he had a better handle on what his supporters felt than the political establishment and pundits. The clearest message that was sent by unwavering support of Trump from his following is that there was a pronounced disconnect between how his supporters viewed the world and how the media and mainstream politicians viewed the same issues. Reality began to set in inside the ranks of the Republican Party that they had to face the possibility that Donald Trump was not going to fade away or destroy his candidacy from a self-inflicted wound. The other factor to be considered by Republican Party insiders was the sheer durability of Trump remaining at the top of their polls for a prolonged period of time would start to create its own gravitational pull.

Trump could no longer be viewed as a sideshow or stunt candidate given his bedrock position atop the polls as others rose and then fell in attempts to make inroads. Trump started to attract looks from some that initially dismissed his run for President as a less than serious undertaking. It seemed that the greatest fear of Republican Party official could be realized as they were being held hostage by a leading candidate they did not want to win the nomination with the threat of an independent run for President on the table if Trump felt he was being treated unfairly by party insiders. In truth the issue that worried Republican Party was lasting brand damage and they did not know how to stem the carnage, because if Trump's views kept him atop his rivals in the polls what did that say about the party as a whole? The surprise should be that the Republican Party was surprised at all by the rise of Donald Trump in their party because they played a large role in creating his legitimacy as a candidate.

Donald Trump deals in extremes and hyperbole. Capitalizing on the fear in his base of ISIS, terrorism and the otherness of individuals from certain locations or of particular religions, Trump to the shock of many and delight of others, proposed a total shutdown of Muslims coming into the United States for a period of time. The idea of banning an entire religion from entering the country was outrageous to those considering it flew in the face of the Constitution of the United States.

After Trump assumed the Presidency many were skeptical he would actually try to ban an entire religion from entering the United States, but he proved them wrong in a surprising way. President Trump tried to enact a form of a Muslim ban through executive order by tying it to a determination by the Obama administration that identified seven countries that were terrorist hotbeds. Trump signed an executive order that banned travel to the United States from the list of countries compiled by the Obama White House and tried to use that as justification. There was one problem with Trump trying to use the Obama policy for cover for his travel ban, Obama's implementation was for visa waivers for people coming from mostly European countries if they had previously visited one of the nations on the list. Trump's executive order was a direct ban on people traveling to the United States directly from the countries on the list. Disorder erupted immediately when the executive order went into effect. Individuals in mid-flight had no idea they could not come into the United States until they landed and were held. Travelers were stranded in airports around the world because they were not allowed to board flight destined for the United States. Some people that were living in the United States flew out of the country for various reasons and were not allowed to return. Green card holders were not even allowed back into the country.

Within short order federal judges placed a hold on Trump's travel ban and deemed it an unconstitutional religious ban although he argued it was a security issue and within the powers of the President to set immigration policy. The 9th U S Circuit Court of Appeals ruled the executive order was unconstitutional and it was eventually withdrawn and replace with a revised executive order and that order was block by a federal judge also and hangs in the balance. President Trump was batting below average on fulfilling his campaign promises.

8– November after election

In August of 2011 both Mitt Romney and Rick Perry sought Donald Trump's endorsement after Trump revealed he had doubts about President Barack Obama being born in the United States and therefore his eligibility to serve as President of the United States under the Constitution. In February of 2012 Donald Trump endorsed Mitt Romney for President and Romney eventually became the Republican nominee to run for President of the United States. Trump began questioning if President Obama was born in the United States on national television in the spring of 2011 before leading Republican Presidential candidates sought his endorsement. Trump went as far as offering to donate $5 million dollars to a charity of President Obama's choice if he published his passport and college application before the end of October 2012. Remember that many of those actions took place after President Obama released his long form Certificate of Live Birth from the State of Hawaii on April 27, 2011, but let us not forget that President Obama's short-form Certification of Live Birth was published online in 2008. Romney accepted Trump's endorsement and did not distance himself based upon the birther issue and that is part of the problem.

Republicans like to play with fire with a wink and a nod. The birther issue and Tea Party movements were watershed moments in modern American politics. Republican candidates and political office holders played fast and loose with issues raised during the height of passion in both cases. The protracted battles over national healthcare, the controversy surrounding the President's birth and rampant anxiety that somehow private gun ownership rights were going to be trampled created an angry firestorm in parts of the Republican base. Much of the anger was reflexive in reaction to the first African American becoming President of the United States signaling a huge shift in the future direction of the United States. Instead of dousing the sparks in the party's base many Republican candidates allowed the embers to become fires and tried to gain momentary political advantage until the situation settled down. In reality the situation didn't settle down, but the lack of success of the agendas those vocal elements supported cause them to become disaffected and go largely silent. The Republican politicians that rode the wave of energy simply moved on and treated the angry groundswell as an anomaly that ran its course, but it was not an anomaly. The people that expended all that energy and displayed all that passion, often in full view of television cameras were still there, still angry and felt dismissed by the very politicians who said they had their backs. Now one out of their own ranks with the money, status and power to get something accomplished stepped onto the stage, threw his hat into the ring for President and it was payback time.

"So you think we're out of touch, irrational and paranoid, but your forgetting one thing, my vote counts the same as that Ivy League graduate or that Wall Street hedge fund manager. My guy,

Trump, has more money than you do and he thinks and talks like we do," could have been the thought process.

Republicans created Trump's legitimacy and now they can't run away from him and his ideas. Trump is resonating and is now the public face of the Republican Party, but not the face they want, but he could be the face they deserve. Due to Trump's statement that parts of London and Pairs were "so radicalized", referring to Islamist extremists, that police could not enter, a petition was posted on the Parliament of The United Kingdom's website to ban Trump from traveling to that country. Citizens of the closest ally of the United States were actively trying to ban the leading Republican candidate for President from entering their country and that was not a good thing.

In typical Trump fashion he had a counter for any potential political damage from a proposed personal ban from the United Kingdom. Trump pledged to sign an executive order, if elected, to impose the death penalty on anyone killing a police officer. Trump understands where his base's hot buttons are located. Trump's supporters were not concerned about the United Kingdom, their concern was making the United States great again so backlash from foreign countries, even allies, did not concern them and Trump knew this. Backlash from outside the borders of the United States against Donald Trump and his policies only served to tighten his grip on his most fervent boosters who felt that part of the United States decline in their eyes was due to what they viewed as too much involvement in international affairs. Donald Trump's vision of a strong, independent and more isolated America had a certain appeal to those with a strong view of the United States as the center of the world. Given the environment of fear of terrorism at home and abroad, the primary concern of many in the United States was to be kept safe from harm from foreign attack at home. Trump did not miscalculate and his pledge to impose the death penalty on cop killers won him the endorsement of a major police union in the battleground state of New Hampshire.

Donald Trump employed classic sales techniques on the campaign trail and selectively took his opponents down one at a time by employing the alternate choice close. One classic example of an alternate choice close is do you want the red sedan with the luxury package or the the blue sedan with the sports package that is $1,000.00 less expensive. Trump used the alternate choice close in the following manner. Would you rather have low energy Jeb Bush or high energy Donald Trump fighting for you? Most of the other politicians competing against Trump didn't realize they were playing a different game than Trump. While the traditional politicians were talking about policy and playing chess, Trump was playing checkers and jumping over them getting crowned. Jeb Bush, Rubio, Cruz and the rest of the Republican field were campaigning for a political office while Donald Trump was selling an idea. Donald Trump was pulling a Barack Obama on the rest of the

Republican political field for President. Hillary Clinton was going over her resume' to be hired as President of the United States with the American public in 2008 while Barack Obama was selling hopes and dreams. As crazy as it sounds Donald Trump was metaphorically the reversed engineered Barack Obama of the 2016 Republican Presidential contest, but he was selling a decidedly different set of hopes and dreams to a much different audience.

President Trump is still the vessel carrying the hopes and dreams of his loyal voting base, but he has not delivered on many promises, but there is one promise he has fulfilled. Trump voters wanted him to shake up Washington DC and he has done that and continues to do so every day. The question Trump voters have to decide is if all Trump is going to do is be a bull in a China shop when do they get tired when their specific reasons for voting for him does not get accomplished. When that factory job does not come back from a foreign country or when a robot is install in a factory and displaces another worker, does another Trump supporter lose faith and abandon him. There is a breaking point when nothing but Presidential turmoil becomes tiresome and will not substitute for progress.

9– November after election

Some might think it is ridiculous to compare the 2008 campaign of Senator Barack Obama and businessman Donald Trump's bid for the 2016 Republican Presidential nomination, but there are similarities. Candidate Obama was selling a vision of a future America that played to the hopes for broader, more inclusive nation with opportunities for more to excel based upon their capabilities. Trump is selling a more exclusive America that is playing to the wishes of his base for a nation with opportunities in this nation reserved for those who are rightfully here and deserve them. Candidate Obama's 2008 campaign slogan was Change. Donald Trump's 2016 campaign slogan was Make America Great Again, which is basically, change back to what we were before.

Trump came out of the blocks and employed a pure strategy of pure offense to the point that the other candidates were set back on their heels. Each time one of Trumps competitors gained traction Trump would shift his focus to that candidate and take them down. Dr. Ben Carson surpassed Trump in the polls and Trump began to punch holes in Carson's background story of youthful violence that played into his narrative of redemption that appealed to evangelicals. Trump's assault on Carson's credibility combined with Carson's stumbles on foreign policy soon resulted in Carson falling behind in later poll rankings. It seemed the next candidate in Trump's sights was Texas Senator Ted Cruz who was rising in the polls and Trump took initial swipes at Cruz over the sensitive issue of support of Ethanol versus oil in Iowa where corn is grown for production of the alternative fuel. Senator Ted Cruz opposed Ethanol subsidies.

With the Iowa caucuses occurring on February 1, 2016 the rest of the Republican field and the party were denying reality if they were still brushing Trump off as a novelty candidate. Less than two months out and the polls gave way to voters selecting delegates and with some early favorites mired in single digit pole numbers panic sat in internally regardless of public statements to the contrary. Before the 2016 Presidential race began it was widely touted that Jeb Bush was the candidate to beat, but he was stuck in single digits in the polls. Some candidates, including Bush, thought that the large number of candidates was fragmenting what the true results would be with a more reasonable sized field of contenders. Those with healthy campaign fund balances dug in for a war of attrition counting on weaker and less well funded candidates withdrawing as their support dried up. The big gamble was a strategy of outlasting their competition banked on picking up their orphaned supporters. It was entirely possible that some supporters of contenders that dropped out would go to Trump in such a volatile race. They were all wrong.

Some political pundits, media and campaign strategists felt that Trump had reached his support ceiling and as other candidates dropped out their support would go to more mainstream contenders. There was one problem with that strategy and that was momentum. If Trump got early wins or splits then he would have passed the test of actually having voters cast votes for him to be President. A supporter casting a vote is like someone spending money to purchase a product after watching a commercial because it is where the rubber meets the road. There was still a long road to someone actually becoming the Republican nominee for President and when the real fight for votes began the gloves would come off. Given the early indications of how Trump would strike back if things got nasty it would be one of the most brutal campaigns ever.

Well things got very nasty and one by one Trump forced his competitors out of the race for the Republican presidential nomination. The tactics of Donald Trump against his competitors were unlike anything seen in politics before. Trump ridiculed his opponents who were United States Senators and former Governors of states. Jeb Bush was tagged as low energy by Trump and it stuck. Jeb Bush dropped out of the race to become the Republican Presidential nominee after losing in the South Carolina primary in February 2016.

Florida Senator Marco Rubio became little Marco and could not shake the disrespectful moniker. Trumps battle with Rubio degenerated to vulgar levels as talk of the size of their hands in relation to their other body parts. Marco Rubio was seen as one of the bright lights for the future of the Republican Party, yet he dropped out of the race to become the Republican Presidential nominee in

94

March 2016 after losing the primary in his home state of Florida.

Senator Ted Cruz was labeled as lying Ted by Trump. Ted Cruz was the only candidate to mount a real challenge to Trump and beat him multiple times. Cruz also exposed the Trump campaigns lack of savvy in navigating back room politics as he outmaneuvered Trump in securing delegates in Colorado. Trump complained that the delegate system was rigged. Cruz fought hard, but dropped out after losing the Indiana primary to Trump in May 2016.

After Cruz dropped out there was only one Republican competitor left in the primary to oppose Trump. Ohio Governor John Kasich was the last man standing trying to prevent Donald Trump from becoming the Republican nominee for President of the United States. One day after Ted Cruz dropped out of the race in May of 2016, Kasich pulled the plug on his campaign. There was nothing stopping Donald Trump from becoming the Republican nominee for President of the United States. Trump went over the 1,237 delegates required as he was unopposed through the rest of the primary season. Trump's next stop would be the Republican National Convention to accept the Republican nomination for President of the United States.

Donald Trump broke all convention and rules on his way to becoming President. Trump defied gravity that would normally bring any other politician down. As President Donald Trump has maintained the same demeanor and issued out new insults and monikers to what he views as adversaries. Trump referred to a federal judge that blocked his travel ban as a "so called judge." Trump referred to Senate Minority Leader Chuck Shumer "Cryin Chuck Shumer" after Shumer shed tears over the confusion caused by Trump's first Muslim travel ban. Trump still went after Senator Elizabeth Warren and referred to her as Pocahontas because of a claim she made in the past that she had Cherokee ancestry that she could not prove. Although Donald Trump's staunchest supporters love his bombastic style, it played better on the campaign trail that is does in the White House.

Trump has offended allies like Mexico, Australia and Germany. Trump has invited the President of the Philippines, Rodrigo Duterte, a self-admitted killer to the White House that has had thousands of his own people killed while prosecuting a brutal war on drugs. Trump is still making friendly overtures to the Russians. Trump referred to North Korean leader Kim Jong Un as a smart cookie. It is obvious that Donald Trump has an affinity with these strongmen type of leaders and sees him as one of them, except we are not in a strongman type of government and that got him in trouble.

The Republican National Convention ran July 18–21, 2016. The Republican National Convention of 2016 was unique due to the absence of so many high profile Republican officials. There were no former Republican Presidents at the convention due to the war Trump had with the Bush family. The only two living former Presidents that are Republicans are George H. W. Bush and his son George W. Bush. The last two Republican Presidential candidates also skipped attending the convention, John McCain and Mitt Romney. Trump tangled with McCain and Romney during the primary going so far as to discount McCain's war service and prisoner of war status. Many other high ranking Republicans were not in attendance at the convention including the governor of the state of Ohio where the Republican National Convention is being held, John Kasich.

The reason so many establishment figures skipped the 2016 Republican National Convention is that the feel their party was high jacked by a pretender in Trump. Trump supported positions that were the opposite of mainstream Republican Party stances for years, before a seemingly miraculous change of heart. Donald Trump was even supportive of his rival to be President of the United States, Hillary Clinton in the past. The truth be told, the primary reason many traditional Republicans were deciding to pass on attending the convention is they did not want to be tied to what they saw as a doomed enterprise. Many Republicans chose to bypass the Cleveland convention had their thoughts set on having clean hands for future political office opportunities beyond the 2016 Presidential election.

The first night of the convention began with the quelling of an attempt by several state delegations to force a roll call vote of adopting rules of the convention. In general the Make America Safe Again theme of the first night was a cavalcade of speakers bashing Democratic Party nominee former Secretary of State Hillary Clinton over Benghazi, ISIS and anything else they could squeeze in.

The second night of the convention featured a speech by Donald Trump's wife, Melania. Donald Trump introduced his wife with a move straight out of his friend Vince McMahon's World Wrestling Enterprise bag of tricks. Standing in silhouette in front of a lit background, Donald Trump walked up to a podiums and twin teleprompters that rose from beneath the stage and introduced his wife. Melania Trump delivered a speech that was very well received until it came to light that it contained parts of First Lady Michele Obama's 2008 Democratic National Convention speech. Charges of plagiarism were denied by the Trump campaign and the story lived on for days until a Trump staffer took the blame for the blunder.

Perhaps the highlight of the convention was delivered by Trump's former Republican primary rival Senator Ted Cruz. Cru walked onto the stage and delivered a dish of cold served revenge to Trump unlike any every seen in a setting such as that. The assembled delegates waited to see if Cruz would endorse a man who retweeted and unflattering photo of Cruz's wife and indicated that Cruz's father was somehow involved in President John F. Kennedy's assassination. Cruz walked out and commanded the stage, camera and convention audience. Cruz spoke Trump's name one time as he congratulated him for winning the nomination. Cruz's speech was broad, sweeping and inclusive, but instead of endorsing Trump he urged convention attendees and all Americans to vote their conscience. Trump supporters in the hall booed Ted Cruz loudly. Cruz's wife was removed from the convention floor because angry Trump supporters were approaching her and behaving aggressively. The next day there were two main stories, Cruz's non-endorsement of Trump and Trump's interview to the New York Times in which he stated that the United States support of our NATO allies may be conditional based upon if they had upheld their obligation. Worldwide reaction was swift and negative from allies. Stay tuned.

On July 21, 2016, Donald J. Trump stepped up to a microphone and gave one of the longest speeches in political convention history. Trump painted a picture of a nation in decline. Trump described a vision of a crime ridden, economically depressed and lawless frontier that he alone can correct. Following Trumps speech, many mainstream pundits characterized it as dark and foreboding with a narcissistic with of himself as the sole available savior.

The next day fact checkers from many of the most respected news organizations in the world debunked many of Trump's claims as not matching the facts or at best selectively chosen to emphasize negativity. The reaction to Trump's speech depended upon the ears that heard it and the eyes that saw it. Trump was not playing to his critics, but to his supporters and potential voters. Donald Trump was not broadcasting, but narrowcasting to his target group. Where Trump detractors saw darkness, his supporters saw light at the end of the tunnel.

Trump's target voters felt the version of America Trump is describing represents them because they are the slice of the country that felt they have been dismissed. The very same flyover states that Presidential candidates say they must win every four years to become President had a large group of people living outside of the urban centers who feel they have been left out and behind. Steel, automobile and textile industries have been decimated. The people supporting Trump saw a vision of a return to blue collar prosperity of the past. Trump went after a black and white version of America where feelings among the attendees attending the Republican National Convention and those mirroring their profile nationwide perceived his speech as uplifting. Where Barack Obama stated that we could do this together, Trump said I alone can fix this.

Unlike Barack Obama who energized a broad coalition to win the Presidency in 2008, Trump is banking on energizing a narrow band of voters with a massive turnout percentage in the right key states. Don't sleep or assume that your version of political logic would prevail, unless you got out and voted in force, President Trump could be in your near future.

Regardless of how he got there, Donald Trump was running to be the President of the United States and there were reasons he was in that position that everyone else missed.

Donald Trump became the Republican nominee for President and of course went on to win the Presidential election. Senator Ted Cruz even with his vocal and forceful protest during the Republican National Convention eventually folded and fell in line behind Trump and campaigned for him. Cruz swallowed his pride and prior insults Trump dished out during the bruising Presidential campaign against his wife and father. Cruz was not alone among Republicans who savaged Trump during the campaign, but later supported and helped him get elected. Republicans were trapped. Donald Trump staged a hostile takeover their party and he was their standard bearer.

When election night arrived and it unbelievably became evident that Trump would become the next President of the United a gleam came to the eyes of Republicans nationwide. Republicans controlled both Houses of Congress and the White House. With Democrats unable to stop them, it appeared to be a slam dunk for Republicans to ram through policies they have wanted to enact for years. There was only on problem, Republicans didn't know how to lead after years of opposing everything. The House of

Representative made a mess out of their attempt to repeal and replace Obamacare. The second huge problem Republican's had was their Republican President, Donald Trump. Donald Trump could not be controlled and brought baggage from the campaign with him in the form of a Russian cloud of suspicion. Trump can't get out of his own way to allow Republican's to enjoy the fruits of their victory.

11– November after election

  *Donald Trump became President of the
United States in large part because Democratic
voter turnout in key states was down from when
President Obama ran. It seems Hillary Clinton
didn't energize and motivate many voters enough
for them get out and vote for her. It seems that some
voters weren't paying attention. Trump repeated his
outrageous and divisive proposals so often that they
seemed normal, but they were far from normal and
after he won, people were marching in the streets in
opposition. It's too late. Sometimes you have to
think of voting as a duty either to get who you want
into office by voting offensively or voting
defensively to keep someone dangerous out of
office. Now here we sit with Donald Trump and all
his divisive promises to his supporters wielding the
power of the Presidency of the United States in his
hands. Almost as frightening is a man some
describe as a White nationalist will be his top
advisor.*

  *All is not lost, but this will be a true test of
our government's checks and balances along with
the strength of the United States Constitution. Be
alert, be vigilant and stay active. Some pondered
how so called God fearing Americans could elevate
a man who had offended so many during his
campaign to the high office of President of the
United States. You have to remember who Trump
offended. Hispanics, Muslims and African
Americans were not Trump's target voters. The
voters that supported Trump agreed with him on*

those groups he offended, so that also won him voters from an ugly fringe that felt emboldened enough to come out of the shadows. Women that were supposed to be repulsed by Trump voted for him in large numbers. Seeing the first woman President in history still would bring your old factory job back to you rural town. Economic outreach by Trump overwhelmed history.

There will be disappointment among Trump voters when his promises go unfulfilled, but he won. Why did so many place a man with Trump's demonstrated flaws in the oval office? Those people were angry, felt ignored and wanted to hit the political status quo so they would pay attention. When you want to hit something, you don't care how the stick looks. Trump was the big stick use to whack the political establishment and everyone is paying attention now.

Everything reviewed prior was written without any knowledge of what would develop after January 20, 2017 when Donald Trump was inaugurated to be the 45th President of the United States. There is no surprise here given what Trump's life and business practices were before he became President. Trump simply moved into the White House with all of the quirks, idiosyncrasies and ego he displayed in his prior life. Trump does not view himself as President to be in service of the American public, but he see himself above the public just like he did in his prior life. Rules that applied to everyone else did not apply to Donald Trump in his life before he became President and now they officially do not apply to him in the role of POTUS.

Donald Trump pointed out to everyone when the issue of business conflicts of interests came up in relation to requests for him to liquidate his business holding or place them in a blind trust that as President he could not have conflicts of interest. As President, Trump can disclose classified information and not face issues as someone below his position would because when the President speaks it, he instantly declassifies it. Donald Trump is the prototype for the one of the most dangerous individuals from a personal history, attitude and temperament standpoint to occupy a position of staggering power like the Presidency of the United States and he proved it in short order.

9

Donald Trump is President of the United States and he did things in a few months that would have heads spinning and screams for impeachment across the board if it was a President Obama or Hillary Clinton in the position doing the same things. Republicans in leadership positions sold their souls in efforts to protect the big rubber stamp they have residing in the White House for the first time in eight years. At some point Trump will cross a line that will not allow Republicans to look the other way. Convenient Christians that excused and ignored Trumps vitriol, amoral attitude and vulgarity will be called into account for allowing their desire to have someone in office that would champion their causes if not their teachings.

Donald Trump is a rampaging rogue bull elephant that has broken loose from his handlers and he is trashing everything in his path. Courts, judges, institutions, the media, lawmakers, allies, classified information and the Constitution of the United States of American, among other things, mean nothing to Donald Trump when it comes to him getting what he wants. Trump is a rogue elephant because he is really not a Republican or Democrat, Trump is just Trump. Trump has always been boastful, flamboyant, hedonistic and most of all, dedicated to his own survival. The fact that Donald Trump values above all his own survival means that everyone in his orbit becomes expendable if it serves his purpose. Almost everyone around Trump have been hung out to dry or thrown under the bus in one way or another except his daughter Ivanka and son-in-law Jared Kusner.

Trump hung his entire communications team and the Vice President out to dry after he fired former FBI Director James Comey with little warning and then threw Deputy Attorney General Rod Rosenstein under the bus. The official line from the White House was that Trump accepted Rosenstein's recommendation that Comey be fired because of how he handled the investigation into former Secretary of State Hillary Clinton's handling of classified information. The official line that President Trump accepted Rosenstein's recommendation to fire Comey was repeated by Trump's communication team and Vice President Pence. The next day Trump hung them all out to dry when he said in a nationally televised interview that he alone decided to fire Comey and had been thinking of doing it for some time regardless of what the Deputy Attorney brought back to him. In one fell swoop, Donald Trump further tarnished the credibility of everyone that carried the official line of why Comey was removed from his position.

Deputy Attorney General Rosenstein felt betrayed by having the firing of Comey publicly pinned solely on him when he knew that was not the case. Trump has thrown numerous other members of the White House inner circle under the bus for various reasons after they defended him from various other accusations only to have him admit to doing what was alleged, often by an early morning tweet. Trump is toxic and individuals that have spent decades building sterling reputations may have them torn down in an instant due to interactions with the sitting President of the United States. Being in the orbit of a President of the United States should enhance ones professional reputation, not destroy it.

So just what will it take to shake Trump sycophants out of their robotic stupor? Those things may have come to pass in a serial fashion and the weight of these events may tip the scales to get things moving towards the beginning of the end for President Donald Trump.

Donald Trump was accustomed to applying leverage to individuals to get what he wanted in his private dealings to the point that it could be considered thuggish behavior. If Trump did everything alleged then he could be on a fast track to eventual ouster. What Trump is alleged to have done combined with what he actually did may not be obstruction of justice but it looks like its twin. All of Trump's most egregious actions revolve around the investigation surrounding potential Trump team ties and possible collusion with Russia to interfere with the 2016 Presidential election.

Reportedly recently sworn in President Donald Trump invited then FBI director James Comey to the White Hosue for dinner and during that time asked the sitting Director of the FBI, a man Trump could fire, for a personal pledge of personal loyalty. Purportedly Comey declined Trumps loyalty pledge request. President Donald Trump desperately wanted the Russian investigation to go away. Trump in particular wanted the investigation into his first National Security Advisor Michael Flynn's Russia investigation to disappear. Acting Attorney General Sally Yates warned the Trump administration that Flynn was subject to blackmail because he lied to team Trump about not having contacts with Russia, but the Russians knew Flynn had discussed sanctions placed upon that country with Flynn. Yates said Russians could blackmail Flynn by threatening to expose the fact he had spoke to him and that was a bad position for a National Security Advisor to be in. Trump kept Flynn in his position for 18 days up he was exposed for his lie in the press and then Trump reluctantly fired him with praise afterward. Flynn was under investigation by the FBI among others.

Trump fired FBI Director James Comey and admitted he had the Russian Investigation into possible coordination of the Trump team with Russia during the campaign on his mind when he made that decision. Fast forward one week after Trump fired the FBI Director and Comey served a cold dish of revenge. Press reports burst upon the scene that rocked the nation. Credible sources related to the press that former FBI Director documented by memo that President Donald Trump asked the Vice President and Attorney General to leave the room when Comey was at the White House. Comey documented that Donald Trump, the President of the United States, asked him in February 2017, if he could end the investigation into General Michael Flynn's Russian ties. President Donald Trump may have committed obstruction of justice if what Comey said was proven true. In true Nixonian fashion Trump twee that Comey better hope the interaction in the White House was not recorded.

Donald Trump was the President of the United States, but he was behaving like a character out of a mob movie by trying to extract personal loyalty out of the Director of the FBI and when he couldn't get his loyalty, Trump leaned on him to drop an ongoing case into his friend, General Michael Flynn, dropped. Like all true bosses, when Trump could not get what he wanted, he personally removed the threat and fired Comey.

Cracks in support began to develop around Trump and finally some Republicans in Congress regained their vision and for the first time in months when they look at the President of the United States, they saw Donald Trump in his true form, Nixon on steroids, but what would they do about it.

Trump was the Republican prize because he was President of the United States and held the golden pen in his hand to sign legislation into law. Republicans in Congress needed to respond to something other than political calculation of how many seats they could lose or if Trump's core supporters still support him despite his actions. Congress is constitutionally an equal branch of government to the Executive branch. Republicans control Congress and they have a duty to act as a check on the President, if required, to protect the nation.

Trump has made us less safe by discouraging our allies from sharing sensitive information on possible terrorist threats due his disclosure of highly sensitive information with Russians in the Oval Office. When will politicians discover true patriotism again? It's time to act because we have a dangerous individual in the White House and he is the President. Calls for impeachment of President Donald Trump began to be spoken out loud.

Impeachment is in Article II of the United States Constitution. Section 4 states:

Section 4
The President, Vice President and all Civil Officers of the United States, shall be removed from Office on Impeachment for, and Conviction of, Treason, Bribery, or other high Crimes and Misdemeanors.

Apparently the pressure of unchecked anarchy in the White House finally forced the hand of the Justice Department as Deputy Attorney General Rod Rosenstein appointed a Special Counsel to oversee the Russia interference into the 2016 U S Presidential election investigation, former FBI Director Robert S. Mueller III. The announcement of the special council is as follows:

Department of Justice
Office of Public Affairs
FOR IMMEDIATE RELEASE
Wednesday, May 17, 2017
Appointment of Special Counsel

Deputy Attorney General Rod J. Rosenstein today announced the appointment of former Department of Justice official and FBI Director Robert S. Mueller III to serve as Special Counsel to oversee the previously-confirmed FBI investigation of Russian government efforts to influence the 2016 presidential election and related matters.

"In my capacity as acting Attorney General, I determined that it is in the public interest for me to exercise my authority and appoint a Special Counsel to assume responsibility for this matter," said Deputy Attorney General Rosenstein. "My decision is not a finding that crimes have been committed or that any prosecution is warranted. I have made no such determination. What I have determined is that based upon the unique circumstances, the public interest requires me to place this investigation under the authority of a person who exercises a degree of independence from the normal chain of command."

Deputy Attorney General Rosenstein added, "Each year, the career professionals of the U.S. Department of Justice conduct tens of thousands of criminal investigations and handle countless other matters without regard to partisan political considerations. I have great confidence in the independence and integrity of our people and our processes. Considering the unique circumstances of this matter, however, I determined that a Special

Counsel is necessary in order for the American people to have full confidence in the outcome. Our nation is grounded on the rule of law, and the public must be assured that government officials administer the law fairly. Special Counsel Mueller will have all appropriate resources to conduct a thorough and complete investigation, and I am confident that he will follow the facts, apply the law and reach a just result."

Special Counsel Mueller has agreed to resign from his private law firm in order to avoid any conflicts of interest with firm clients or attorneys.

Source:https://www.justice.gov/opa/pr/appointment -special-counsel

As the saying goes, things got real for one President Donald John Trump. Trump has proved he is truly Nixon on steroids as we are in Watergate territory in less than four months after he took office, not years. The ultimate irony is that two of the institutions Trump went to war with joined forces to bring him to this point, the U S intelligence community and the media, just like Nixon. Just like Nixon went up against the FBI and lost, Trump may suffer the same fate. Donald Trump does not seem to be a student of history and tragically, may be doomed to repeat it.

I know you're busy every day trying to keep your life together, but watch this space.

Stay woke!

About The Author

ESSENCE® bestselling author D.T. Pollard lives in the Dallas/Fort Worth, TX area. He is married and has one son.

Other works
By
D T Pollard
Rooftop Diva – A Novel of Triumph
After Katrina (fiction)
Fools' Heaven – Love, Lust and
Death Beyond the Pulpit (fiction)
TARP TOWN U S A – The
Recession That Saved America
OBAMA GUILTY OF BEING PRESIDENT
WHILE BLACK
Vampire Sapien
The Mark Unmasked
Publish Free For Kindle Today
Sell Worldwide Tomorrow
World Wide Nuclear Power Plant Guide
Unemployed But Not Destroyed
Vulture Capitalism
Whitney Houston – Poems for Whitney
Whitney Amy Michael Elvis
The Good Old Girls Club
President Obama – Diary of Disrespect
Who
Who Moved My Ocean – Avoid The Shrinking Job
Trap
Mitt Romney's America – No Trespassing By The
47%

Romnesia – How Dangerous Is It
Obama 2.0
Carnage Control
Gold Digger's Grave
Things You Can't Tell Mama – The Pastor's Wife
Things You Can't Tell Mama – Her Man Was Once
Yours
Things You Can't Tell Mama – Her Blond Best
Friend
Things You Can't Tell Mama - Mr. Taboo
Things You Can't Tell Mama – The Prophetess
Affair
Things You Can't Tell Mama–Your Best Friend's
Mother
Things You Can't Tell Mama – The President's Sex
Tape
Things You Can't Tell Mama – Anthology
Confessions of a Single Black Woman
Tiberius – Rap's Rainmaker
Things you Can't Tell Mama – The Pastor's Wife 2
Mommy Porn
Jacob's Cabin
The Pastor's Lover
Side Piece
Side Piece 2 – Amber Alarm
Hero In The Hood
The Pastor's Lover 2
She Twerks Hard For The Money
The Pastor's Lover 3
Forget Big Brother We Tell DAD Everything
The Pastor's Wife 3
Hoe Hoe Hoe Merry Christmas
Ghetto Tony and White Trash Tina

Fifty Shades of Plaid
Grandma Does It Better
Keisha's Mama Is So Fine
Less Pretty
Pretty For A Dark Skinned Woman
Massive Monroe
The Pastor's Lover 4 – The Pastor's Wife 4
The Obituary of Gut Bucket Johnson
Forget Big Brother – We Tell DAD Everything
Unreal Housewives of South Dallas
Liquid Memories: You Can Live Forever
Gold Digger's Game
Ebola – Partying With Grace
THOT On The Beach
What Would Dr King Think About Today's Black America
Blackphobia - Bluephobia
Your Best Friend's Mother 2 – Lust In London
Secrets of a Baby Mama 2

www.ingramcontent.com/pod-product-compliance
Lightning Source LLC
Chambersburg PA
CBHW050534280326
41933CB00011B/1579